Crystallization-Study
of
**Daniel
and
Zechariah**

Volume Two

The Holy Word for Morning Revival

Witness Lee

Living Stream Ministry
Anaheim, CA • www.lsm.org

© 2013 Living Stream Ministry

First Edition, February 2013.

ISBN 978-0-7363-6416-4

Published by

Living Stream Ministry
2431 W. La Palma Ave., Anaheim, CA 92801 U.S.A.
P. O. Box 2121, Anaheim, CA 92814 U.S.A.

Printed in the United States of America

13 14 15 16 / 5 4 3 2 1

2012 Winter Training

CRYSTALLIZATION-STUDY OF DANIEL AND ZECHARIAH

Contents

Preface

1. This book is intended as an aid to believers in developing a daily time of morning revival with the Lord in His word. At the same time, it provides a limited review of the winter training held December 24-29, 2012, in Anaheim, California, on the "Crystallization-study of Daniel and Zechariah." Through intimate contact with the Lord in His word, the believers can be constituted with life and truth and thereby equipped to prophesy in the meetings of the church unto the building up of the Body of Christ.

2. The entire content of this book is taken from *Crystallization-study Outlines: Daniel and Zechariah,* the text and footnotes of the Recovery Version of the Bible, selections from the writings of Witness Lee and Watchman Nee, and *Hymns,* all of which are published by Living Stream Ministry.

3. The book is divided into weeks. One training message is covered per week. Each week presents first the message outline, followed by six daily portions, a hymn, and then some space for writing. The training outline has been divided into days, corresponding to the six daily portions. Each daily portion covers certain points and begins with a section entitled "Morning Nourishment." This section contains selected verses and a short reading that can provide rich spiritual nourishment through intimate fellowship with the Lord. The "Morning Nourishment" is followed by a section entitled "Today's Reading," a longer portion of ministry related to the day's main points. Each day's portion concludes with a short list of references for further reading and some space for the saints to make notes concerning their spiritual inspiration, enlightenment, and enjoyment to serve as a reminder of what they have received of the Lord that day.

4. The space provided at the end of each week is for composing a short prophecy. This prophecy can be composed by considering all of our daily notes, the "harvest" of our inspirations during the week, and preparing a main point with

some sub-points to be spoken in the church meetings for the organic building up of the Body of Christ.

5. Following the last week in this volume, we have provided reading schedules for both the Old and New Testaments in the Recovery Version with footnotes. These schedules are arranged so that one can read through both the Old and New Testaments of the Recovery Version with footnotes in two years.

6. As a practical aid to the saints' feeding on the Word throughout the day, we have provided verse cards at the end of the volume, which correspond to each day's Scripture reading. These may be cut out and carried along as a source of spiritual enlightenment and nourishment in the saints' daily lives.

7. *Crystallization-study Outlines: Daniel and Zechariah* was compiled by Living Stream Ministry from the writings of Witness Lee and Watchman Nee. The outlines, footnotes, and cross-references in the Recovery Version of the Bible are by Witness Lee. All of the other references cited in this publication are from the published ministry of Witness Lee and Watchman Nee.

Winter Training
(December 24-29, 2012)

CRYSTALLIZATION-STUDY
OF DANIEL AND ZECHARIAH

Banners:

We need a vision to see that the excellent Christ,
the centrality and universality of God's economy,
is the precious and preeminent One in God's move,
that as the Son of Man in ascension
He has received dominion and a kingdom, and
that His coming will terminate human government
and bring in the eternal kingdom of God.

The overcomers as the shining stars
are a duplication of Christ as the living Star,
and they are the messengers of the churches,
those who are one with Christ as the Messenger of God
and who possess the present Christ
as the living and fresh message
sent by God to His people.

Christ is everything for God's building,
and as the engraved stone with seven eyes,
the topstone of grace,
He is now transfusing what He is
and what He has accomplished into our being
so that, by becoming the same as He is
in life and nature but not in the Godhead,
we may be His reproduction
for the building of the temple of God.

In His heavenly ministry
Christ was designated to be a kingly High Priest
according to the order of Melchizedek
to minister Himself as the processed Triune God
into us in order to be our daily life supply
and enjoyment for our nourishment, refreshment,
sustenance, comfort, and strengthening,
so that we may be saved to the uttermost for
the building up of the church as the temple of God.

Christ as Everything
for the Building of the Temple of God

Scripture Reading: Ezra 5:1-2; Zech. 1:1, 7-17; 2:1-13; 3:9; 4:7; 6:12-13

Day 1   I. **The temple of God is the goal of God's eternal economy (Eph. 1:10; 3:9; 1 Tim. 1:4; John 2:19-22; 1 Cor. 3:16-17; Eph. 2:21; Rev. 21:2, 22):**

   A. The temple in the Old Testament typifies both the individual Christ and the corporate Christ, the church (1 Kings 6:1-2):

      1. The temple first typifies the individual, incarnated Christ as the dwelling place of God on earth (Col. 2:9; John 1:14; 2:19-22).

      2. The temple also typifies the corporate Christ, the church, as the enlarged temple, the unique building of God in the universe (Matt. 12:6; 1 Cor. 3:16-17; 12:12; Eph. 2:21).

   B. The church is the temple of God; as such, it is the sanctuary of the holy God, the temple in which the Spirit of God dwells (1 Cor. 3:16-17):

      1. The temple of God in verse 16 refers to the believers collectively in a certain locality, whereas the temple of God in verse 17 refers to all the believers universally.

      2. The unique spiritual temple of God in the universe has its expression in many localities on earth; each expression is the temple of God in that locality (Eph. 2:21-22).

   C. There is no temple in the New Jerusalem, for the Lord God the Almighty and the Lamb are its temple (Rev. 21:22):

      1. In the new heaven and new earth the temple of God will be enlarged into a city.

      2. The city as a whole will be the Holy of Holies; hence, there will be no temple in it (v. 16).

Day 2   II. **The center, the aim, and the goal of Satan's struggle against God are related to the temple of God
(Matt. 16:18; John 2:19-22; Dan. 11:36-45):**

A. God desires to have a place on earth for His people
to worship Him, as a testimony that He still has
an interest on this earth (1 Kings 7:51; 8:10-11).

B. Satan is always struggling to destroy the temple
of God (2 Kings 25:1-4, 9; Ezra 5:13; 6:15; Dan.
11:21-35; Matt. 22:7; 24:1-2, 15; 2 Thes. 2:3-4, 8;
Rev. 11:1-2).

III. **Zechariah prophesied to help the returned
Israelites in the work of building the temple;
the rebuilding work continued through the
encouragement and help of the prophesying
of the prophets Haggai and Zechariah (Ezra
5:1-2):**

A. Zechariah was born of a priestly family in captivity; he was first a priest, and then he became
a prophet (Neh. 12:1, 4, 12, 16; Zech. 1:1).

B. Because his ministry sprang from and was based
on his priesthood, Zechariah spoke very much
concerning Christ; he did not predict anything
but Christ, and all he spoke about was Christ,
because he was a priest contacting the Lord all
the time (9:9; 11:7, 12-13; 12:10; 14:17).

IV. **The book of Zechariah reveals that Christ is
everything for the recovery of the building
of God's house, the temple of God:**

A. We need the heavenly vision to see the things
concerning Christ related to the recovery of the
building of the temple of God (6:12-13).

Day 3   B. In Zechariah 1:7-17 we see the vision of a man
riding on a red horse and standing among the
myrtle trees:

1. This man is the Angel of Jehovah, Christ in
His humanity (v. 11; Exo. 3:2a, 4-6, 13-15;
23:20; 32:34).

2. The red horse signifies Christ's swift move
in His redemption, accomplished through

the shedding of His blood (Zech. 1:8; Eph. 1:7; 1 Pet. 1:18-19).

3. The redeeming Christ, as a man and as the Angel of Jehovah, was sent by God to be with the humiliated yet precious people of Israel (myrtle trees) in their captivity (Zech. 1:8).

4. Christ interceded for those in captivity, and Jehovah answered His prayer, saying, "I return to Jerusalem with compassions; My house will be built in it, declares Jehovah of hosts" (vv. 12, 16).

C. In 2:1-13 we see the vision of a man with a measuring line in His hand:

1. This man is Christ in His humanity as the Angel of Jehovah, the One speaking with Zechariah (vv. 1a, 2).

2. The man with the measuring line intended to measure Jerusalem so that Jehovah might repossess it after the seventy years of Israel's captivity (vv. 2, 4b).

Day 4

3. In verse 8 both *He* and *Me* refer to Jehovah of hosts:

a. This means that Jehovah of hosts is the Sender and the sent One (vv. 9, 11).

b. Jehovah is the Triune God; in verse 8 one of the three in the Godhead, referred to as "He," sent another of the three, referred to as "Me."

c. The Sender is surely the Father, and the sent One is the Son (John 5:36b; 6:57a; 8:16).

d. "After the glory"—after the return of the captives—the Triune God decided that the Father would send the Son against the nations who plundered Israel; both the Father and the Son are Jehovah (Zech. 2:8).

D. In Zechariah Christ is revealed as the stone with seven eyes (3:9), the topstone (4:7), and the Shoot that will build the temple of Jehovah (6:12-13).

E. In Zechariah's prophecy Christ was sent to Israel as their King in a lowly form (9:9-10) and as their Shepherd to feed them (11:7), but He was detested (v. 8), sold (vv. 12-13), attacked (13:7), and pierced (12:10), and thereby accomplished redemption for them (13:1; 1:8; 3:9).

F. Eventually, Christ will fight for Israel to deliver them out of the hand of Antichrist for their household salvation (12:1—14:7, 12-15), and in the restoration Christ will be King over the earth (vv. 8-11, 16-21).

Day 5 V. As the development of the prophecy concerning Christ in Zechariah, Matthew and 1 Corinthians reveal that the all-inclusive Christ is everything for the building of the church as the temple of God:

A. Matthew reveals that for the building of the church (16:18), Christ is the King (2:1-2; 21:5), the Son of the living God (16:16), the Son of Man (8:20; 11:19), the Baptizer (3:11), the light (4:12-16), the Physician (9:12), the Bridegroom (v. 15), the unfulled cloth (v. 16), the new wine (v. 17), the Shepherd (v. 36), the Lord of the harvest (v. 38), the Friend of sinners (11:19a), wisdom (v. 19b), the One who gives rest (vv. 28-30), the real David (12:3), the One greater than the temple (v. 6), the greater Jonah (vv. 39-41), the One greater than Solomon (v. 42), the bread and crumbs under the table (15:26-27), and the resurrected One in His humanity with all authority in heaven and on earth (28:18-19).

B. First Corinthians reveals that for the building of the church as the temple of God (3:16-17), the Body-Christ (12:12), Christ is the believers' portion (1:2), God's power and God's wisdom as righteousness, sanctification, and redemption to us (vv. 24, 30), the Lord of glory (2:7-8), the depths of God (v. 10), the unique foundation of God's building (3:11), our Passover (5:7), the unleavened bread (v. 8), the spiritual food, the spiritual drink, and the spiritual rock (10:3-4), the Head (11:3), the Body (12:12), the firstfruits (15:20, 23), the second man (v. 47), and the last Adam, who became the life-giving Spirit (v. 45b) so that we may receive Him as our everything for the church.

Day 6 **VI. For the building of the church as the temple of God, we need certain crucial experiences of Christ:**

A. For the building of the church as the temple of God, we need to experience Christ as the foundation, the One who holds and supports the entire church (3:11).

B. For the building of the church as the temple of God, we need to experience Christ as the cornerstone (Acts 4:11; Eph. 2:20; 1 Pet. 2:6).

C. For the building of the church as the temple of God, we need to experience Christ as the topstone, as grace from God to us to be the covering of God's building (Zech. 4:7; 1 Cor. 15:10).

D. For the building of the church as the temple of God, we need to experience Christ as the precious building materials—gold, silver, and precious stones (3:12a).

E. For the building of the church as the temple of God, we need to experience Christ as wisdom to us from God (1:30).

F. For the building of the church as the temple of God, we need to experience Christ in the power of His resurrection (Phil. 3:10-11).

G. For the building of the church as the temple of God, we need to experience Christ in His death (v. 10; S. S. 4:6).

H. For the building of the church as the temple of God, we need to experience Christ in His love (2 Cor. 5:14; Eph. 3:17-19; 4:16).

Morning Nourishment

1 Cor. **Do you not know that you are the temple of God,**
3:16 **and *that* the Spirit of God dwells in you?**
Rev. **And I saw no temple in it, for the Lord God the**
21:22 **Almighty and the Lamb are its temple.**

The temple replaced the tabernacle as God's dwelling on earth. The temple first signifies the incarnated Christ, the embodiment of God (Col. 2:9), as God's dwelling on the earth (John 2:19-21; 1:14). It also signifies the church, including all the believers, the members of Christ, as the enlargement of Christ to be God's dwelling on the earth (1 Cor. 3:16-17; 6:19; Eph. 2:21-22). Christ and the church are one, Christ being the Head and the church being the Body (Eph. 1:22-23; Col. 1:18a). The Body is the enlargement of the Head for God's dwelling. Hence, God's dwelling in Christ is God's dwelling in the church. (1 Kings 6:1, footnote 2)

Today's Reading

Solomon typifies Christ (Matt. 12:42) in speaking God's word of wisdom (13:35) and in building the church as the temple of God (16:18; 1 Cor. 3:16; Eph. 2:21-22), and the temple typifies Christ (Matt. 12:6) and the church as the unique building of God in the universe. These two—Christ and His Body, the church—are the center, the reality, and the goal of God's eternal economy. (*Life-study of 1 & 2 Kings,* p. 41)

In the New Testament, Christ is the tabernacle of God and the temple of God (John 1:14; 2:21)....Christ has been enlarged, and the enlarged Christ is the church as God's enlarged temple. The church as the enlargement of Christ is God's enlarged temple, His dwelling place. In 1 Corinthians 3:16 Paul said that the believers corporately are the temple of God; in Ephesians 2:22 he said that we are being built together into a spiritual dwelling place of God; and in 1 Timothy 3:15 he said that the church is the house of the living God. First, God is in Christ. When we call on the name of Christ, we get God. Furthermore, God is in the church. The church, of course, is not a physical building. We believers are the church. (*Life-study of the Psalms,* p. 155)

The temple of God [in 1 Corinthians 3:16] refers to the believers collectively in a certain locality,...whereas the temple of God in verse 17 refers to all the believers universally. The unique spiritual temple of God in the universe has its expression in many localities on earth. Each expression is the temple of God in that locality.

The temple of God is the explanation of God's building in verse 9. God's building is not an ordinary building; it is the sanctuary of the holy God, the temple in which the Spirit of God dwells. We, the builders of such a holy temple, should realize this, that we may be careful to build not with the worthless materials of wood, grass, and stubble but with the precious materials of gold, silver, and precious stones, which correspond with God's nature and economy. (1 Cor. 3:16, footnote 1)

Both the tabernacle and the temple typify the New Jerusalem. In the new heavens and the new earth, the temple will be enlarged into a city, the New Jerusalem. There will be no temple in the New Jerusalem because the temple will be enlarged into a city (Rev. 21:22). Today God's dwelling can be likened to a house, but in eternity God's dwelling will be a city. The house will be enlarged into a city. (*Three Aspects of the Church, Book 1: The Meaning of the Church*, p. 200)

This temple (v. 22), according to the original text, does not refer to the entire temple including the Holy Place and the Holy of Holies; rather, it refers to the inner temple, the Holy of Holies. This inner temple is the almighty God and Christ as the Lamb, signifying that God and Christ Themselves will be the place in which we serve God in the new heaven and new earth. The holy city as the tabernacle of God (Rev. 21:3) is for God to dwell in, and God and the Lamb as the temple are for us to dwell in (cf. Psa. 27:4; 92:13). In the new heaven and new earth, the holy city New Jerusalem will be a mutual dwelling place for both God and man for eternity. (*Truth Lessons—Level One*, vol. 2, pp. 106-107)

Further Reading: God's New Testament Economy, ch. 37; *Three Aspects of the Church, Book 1: The Meaning of the Church*, ch. 17

Enlightenment and inspiration: _____

_____

_____

_____

Morning Nourishment

Zech. ...Thus speaks Jehovah of hosts, saying, Here is a
6:12-13 man, whose name is the Shoot; and he will shoot forth
from his place and will build the temple of Jehovah.
Indeed,...he will bear majesty and will sit and rule on
his throne; and he will be a priest on his throne; and
the counsel of peace will be between the two of them.

The first temple was built by Solomon, and that temple was
destroyed by Nebuchadnezzar. Then after seventy years, Cyrus
the king of Persia released the captives of Israel to return to their
fathers' land to rebuild the temple. Eventually, Antiochus Epi-
phanes, a descendant of the king of the north, utterly desecrated
the temple, profaning it with idolatry, fornication, and unclean
offerings. The Maccabees defeated this king and cleansed the
temple. That cleansing was a justification, declaring that the temple was the holy place for God's people to worship Him. After
Christ's death, Titus came with the Roman army and destroyed
the temple again in A.D. 70. According to the Bible, there will be a
fourth destruction of the temple by Antichrist in the middle of
the last seven years of this age.

All these cases show us that the center, the aim, and the goal of
Satan's struggle against God is related to the temple. God desires to
have a place on earth for His people to worship Him, as a testimony
that He still has an interest on this earth. But Satan is always
struggling to destroy this place. (*Life-study of Daniel*, pp. 104-105)

Today's Reading

The rebuilding work [of the temple] continued through the encouragement and help of the prophesying of the prophets Haggai
and Zechariah (Ezra 5:1-2). In God's theocratic administration
among the people of Israel, there were three offices: the priests, the
kings, and the prophets....The rebuilding of the temple was accomplished through the priesthood of Joshua and the authority of
Zerubbabel, the governor of Judah (Hag. 1:1). In the building of the
recovered temple both Joshua and Zerubbabel became somewhat
weak and discouraged. Therefore, God used the prophets Haggai

and Zechariah to speak for Him and to strengthen and encourage Joshua and Zerubbabel. (Ezra 5:1, footnote 1)

Zechariah was born of a priestly family in captivity (Neh. 12:1, 4, 12, 16). He was first a priest, and then he became a prophet. He returned to Judah with Zerubbabel at the time of the prophet Haggai in about 520 B.C. (Ezra 5:1). (Zech. 1:1, footnote 2)

[Zechariah's] prophecy was based upon his priesthood. He spoke very much concerning Christ because his ministry sprang from the priesthood. Today in the Lord's recovery, we need the prophets such as Haggai to strengthen us, warn us, and stir us, but we need prophets such as Zechariah even more....We need the prophets who are the real priests, who have living contact with the Lord and who know something of Christ....All [Zechariah] spoke about was Christ, because he was a priest contacting the Lord all the time.

The ministry of the prophet Zechariah is a ministry concerning Christ, showing that in God's recovery, Christ must have the first place. In the books of the recovery—Ezra, Nehemiah, Haggai, and Zechariah—eventually there is nothing but Christ. The recovery is the recovery of the building of God's house, but it is for Christ.

Brothers and sisters, we must see that this mystery is the mystery of Christ. In the recovery of the Lord's house today, we do not need the prophets like Haggai so much. Yet today nearly all the prophets are like Haggai. Have you heard some prophecy about Christ as God's mystery? This is the problem today. There are too many Haggais and hardly any Zechariahs. Haggai only opens the way for the prophecy, and Zechariah follows. In the recovery of the local churches, we need more prophecies like Zechariah's, more prophecies about Christ. Today we rarely hear the voice of Zechariah, because it is mysterious; it is something that is not according to the human concept. We need the heavenly vision to see the things concerning Christ related to the recovery of the building of God's house. (*The Recovery of God's House and God's City,* pp. 47-48, 55, 49)

Further Reading: The Recovery of God's House and God's City, chs. 4-5

Enlightenment and inspiration: _____
_____
_____
_____

Morning Nourishment

Zech.   **I saw during the night, and behold, a man was riding**
1:8   **upon a red horse; and He was standing among the**
     myrtle trees that were in the bottoms; and behind
     Him there were red, reddish-brown, and white horses.
  16   **Therefore thus says Jehovah, I return to Jerusa-**
     lem with compassions; My house will be built in it,
     declares Jehovah of hosts, and a measuring line
     will be stretched over Jerusalem.

In order that Zechariah might strengthen the rebuilding work of the holy temple by foretelling its success, God gave him a series of eight visions in the beginning of the prophecies in his book. The first vision was of a man riding upon a red horse and standing among the myrtle trees (the people of Israel) that were in the bottoms (the land of captivity) (1:7-17). The one riding on a red horse denotes the Angel of Jehovah,...Christ. The angel stood in the bottoms, where God's people were kept in captivity, staying with them and interceding for their return. God answered that He was jealous for Jerusalem with a great jealousy, and He was very displeased with the nations which helped forward the affliction; He would grant mercies that His house might be rebuilt and a line stretched upon Jerusalem. (*Truth Lessons—Level One*, vol. 2, pp. 8-9)

Today's Reading

The man [in Zechariah 1:8] is the Angel of Jehovah (v. 11), Christ in His humanity. The Angel of Jehovah is Jehovah Himself as the Triune God (Exo. 3:2a, 4-6, 13-15). He is also Christ as the embodiment of the Triune God (Col. 2:9) and as the sent One of God (John 5:36-38; 6:38-39). The Angel of Jehovah is also the Angel of God who escorted and protected Israel on their way from Egypt to the promised land (Exo. 23:20; 32:34...). (Zech. 1:8, footnote 1)

[The] myrtle trees signify the humiliated yet precious people of Israel in their captivity. The redeeming Christ, as a man and as the Angel of Jehovah, the embodiment of the Triune God, was sent by God to be with the humiliated people of Israel in their captivity. Christ's standing among the myrtle trees that were in the bottoms means that He remained strongly among the captured Israel in the lowest part of the valley in their humiliation. As the One on the red horse, Christ, the redeeming One, was Israel's patron, ready to do anything for them swiftly in order to care for them in their captivity. Christ maintained Israel in their captivity that He might eventually be born into humanity through Israel to accomplish God's eternal economy. (Zech. 1:8, footnote 3)

In [Zechariah 1:12] we see that the Angel of Jehovah interceded for Israel. "Then the Angel of Jehovah answered and said, O Jehovah of hosts, how long will You not have compassion on Jerusalem and on the cities of Judah, with which You have been indignant for these seventy years?"

[In verse 16] to measure is to possess. For Jehovah to cause a measuring line to be stretched over Jerusalem means that He will possess that city. For seventy years Jerusalem was given up by God. Now He was coming back to repossess the city, so He sent someone to measure it. In verse 17 Jehovah went on to say, "My cities will again overflow with good, and Jehovah will again comfort Zion and will again choose Jerusalem." This is the way Christ's prayer for Israel was answered by God.

In [chapter 2] Zechariah saw a vision of a man with a measuring line in His hand. "I lifted up my eyes and I looked, and there was a man, and in His hand was a measuring line. And I said, Where are you going? And He said to me, To measure Jerusalem; to see how great its breadth is and how great its length is" (vv. 1-2)....This man is Christ in His humanity as the Angel of Jehovah, the One speaking with Zechariah (vv. 1a, 2-3a; cf. Ezek. 40:3; Zech. 1:9-11)....The man with the measuring line intended to measure Jerusalem for the purpose that Jehovah may repossess it (Zech. 2:2, 4b). Jerusalem was given up by God for the seventy years of captivity. After the captivity, God came back to Jerusalem to measure it for His possession. (*Life-study of Zechariah*, pp. 9-10, 13-14)

Further Reading: Life-study of Zechariah, msgs. 1-2

Enlightenment and inspiration: _____

_____

_____

_____

Morning Nourishment

Zech.   For thus says Jehovah of hosts, After the glory He
2:8-9   has sent Me against the nations who plunder you;
    for he who touches you touches the pupil of His eye.
    For I am now waving My hand over them, and they
    will be plunder for those who served them; and
    you will know that Jehovah of hosts has sent Me.

Zechariah 2:8 says, "Thus says Jehovah of hosts, After the glory He has sent Me against the nations who plunder you; for he who touches you touches the pupil of His eye." What is meant by the expression "after the glory"? It refers to after the return of the captives. In the seventy years of captivity, the glory was absent from the center of Jerusalem. But when the children of Israel returned to Jerusalem, the glory also returned. Although Joshua and Zerubbabel were godly, many of the others who returned to Jerusalem from Babylon were not. Nevertheless, in the sight of God, their return was a glory. Therefore, "after the glory" means "after the return."

The first part of verse 8 says, "Thus says Jehovah of hosts, After the glory He has sent Me." Who is the *He,* and who is the *Me?* The *He* refers to God, Jehovah of hosts, and the *Me* refers also to Jehovah of hosts. Jehovah of hosts sent Jehovah of hosts. This means that Jehovah of hosts is the Sender and the One sent. In the Old Testament, *Jehovah* is a divine title that refers to the Triune God. (*Life-study of Zechariah,* pp. 15-16)

Today's Reading

In Zechariah 2:8 one of the three in the Godhead sent another of the three. The Sender is called *He,* and the sent One is called *Me.* Surely the *He* refers to the Father, and the *Me,* to the Son. After the glory, the Triune God decided to do something marvelous. The decision was that the Father would send the Son....Both the Father and the Son are Jehovah.

Christ as the One sent by Jehovah of hosts and as the Sender, Jehovah of hosts, will be against the nations who plunder the people of Zion and touch them as the pupil of His eye. (*Life-study of Zechariah,* p. 17)

[In Zechariah, Christ is unveiled as the topstone of grace, a stone with seven eyes (4:7; 3:9)]. Additional...prophecies concerning Christ are: "I am about to bring forth My servant, the shoot" (Zech. 3:8); and "Here is a *man,* whose name is the Shoot; and he will shoot forth from his place and will build the temple of Jehovah. Indeed, it is he who will build the temple of Jehovah; and he will bear majesty and will sit and rule on his throne; and he will be a priest on his throne" (Zech. 6:12-13). All these designations refer to Christ. He is God's Servant, He is a man, and He is called the Shoot. He will build the temple of Jehovah, and He will sit on the throne and rule and be a Priest. (*Concerning the Person of Christ,* p. 23)

Chapters 9 through 11 of Zechariah unveil Christ in a very intimate way. The center of the prophecies in these chapters is Christ as the rejected Messiah. In chapter 9 Christ came and entered into Jerusalem as the King in a lowly form. Then chapter 10 reveals this kind, intimate, and gentle One as the Shepherd coming in His loving visitation to Israel. When He was thirty years of age, He came forth to shepherd the people. During the three and a half years of His ministry on earth, He ministered the spiritual supply to God's chosen people. The time of His ministry was a time of shepherding, and many were helped by His shepherding.

The book of Zechariah does not stress Christ's being or His working. Rather, it reveals Christ as the One who was sent to Israel as their King in a lowly form but was detested, sold, attacked, and pierced, and thereby accomplished redemption for them. Christ as the Angel of Jehovah was with them in their captivity. Eventually, Christ will fight for Israel and will be King over all the earth. (*Life-study of Zechariah,* pp. 64, 5)

Further Reading: Life-study of Zechariah, msg. 3; *Truth Lessons—Level One,* vol. 2, lsn. 13

Enlightenment and inspiration: _____
_____
_____
_____

Morning Nourishment

Matt. **And Simon Peter answered and said, You are the**
16:16 **Christ, the Son of the living God.**
1 Cor. **But of Him you are in Christ Jesus, who became**
1:30 **wisdom to us from God: both righteousness and**
sanctification and redemption.

The fourteen chapters of Zechariah are divided into two sections: the first eight chapters are one section, and the last six are another. In the first section, there are eight visions, in which the prophet Zechariah saw the things of Christ related to the recovery of God's building; in the last section, Zechariah prophesies about Christ in the future, after the recovery of the temple. (*The Recovery of God's House and God's City,* p. 45)

Today's Reading

In Matthew 21:1-11 Christ is presented as the King, in particular, as the meek King. Shortly before the end of His life, the Lord Jesus entered Jerusalem as the King.

In Matthew 16:16-19 we see that the Lord Jesus is the Christ, the Son of the living God. The revelation here is crucial, for it concerns God's economy, His eternal purpose....Wherever we go, we must preach and teach the Christ and the Son of the living God so that many more sons may be produced to be the members of the church, the Body of Christ.

We may experience and enjoy Christ not only as God but also as a man—the Son of Man (Matt. 4:4; 19:28; 26:64; 24:37, 39, 44). However, not many Christians have a particular and fine experience of Christ as a man.

Matthew 9:10-13 indicates that we also may experience and enjoy Christ as the Physician. In calling people to follow Him for the kingdom, the Lord Jesus ministered as a Physician, not as a Judge....He came to minister as a Physician, to heal, recover, enliven, and save us, that we might be reconstituted to be His new and heavenly citizens, with whom He is establishing His heavenly kingdom on this corrupted earth.

Matthew 25:1 is a further word concerning the Lord Jesus as

the Bridegroom. This verse reveals that the Lord will come back as the Bridegroom, as the pleasant and attractive person. (*The Conclusion of the New Testament,* pp. 2816, 2808-2809, 2771, 2782-2783)

First Corinthians 1:2 speaks of calling on the name of "our Lord Jesus Christ,...who is theirs and ours." Nowhere else in the New Testament can we find such an expression. We need to call on the Lord Jesus because He is our portion [for us to enjoy] (Col. 1:12). (*The Enjoyment of Christ for the Body in 1 Corinthians,* p. 11)

In 1 Corinthians 10:3 and 4 we see Christ as our spiritual food, our spiritual drink, and our spiritual rock. Christ is the manna, and He is the living water that flows out of the cleft rock. Today our daily food and drink are Christ. The living water flowing out of the rock indicates that the rock is the source of supply....Our supply is Christ, and our source of supply is also Christ. This source being a rock signifies that Christ is altogether dependable; we can rely on Him. Christ is our spiritual food, our spiritual drink, and our reliable source of supply, which always follows us.

First Corinthians 11:3 reveals that Christ is the Head, and 12:12 reveals that He is also the Body. Christ is both the Head and the Body, the church. Therefore, in the church there is no natural person, but Christ is all and in all (Col. 3:10-11).

First Corinthians 15 reveals four more aspects of Christ—the firstfruits (v. 20), the second man (v. 47), the last Adam (v. 45), and the life-giving Spirit (v. 45). Thus, Christ is first, second, and last. This indicates that Christ is every positive thing in the universe.... God's power, God's wisdom, righteousness, sanctification, redemption, the depths of God, our foundation, the Passover, the Feast of Unleavened Bread, our spiritual food, our spiritual drink, our rock, the Head, the Body, the firstfruits, the second man, and the last Adam are all in the life-giving Spirit. (*The Recovery of Christ as Everything in the Church,* p. 25)

Further Reading: The Conclusion of the New Testament, msgs. 267-272; *The Enjoyment of Christ for the Body in 1 Corinthians,* chs. 1-3

Enlightenment and inspiration: _____

_____

_____

_____

Morning Nourishment

1 Cor. For another foundation no one is able to lay be-
3:11 sides that which is laid, which is Jesus Christ.
Phil. To know Him and the power of His resurrection
3:10 and the fellowship of His sufferings, being conformed to His death.

When we get back to the proper ground, we must pray that
such a foundation [in 1 Corinthians 3:11] will be laid....It is
not a matter of imitating but of being filled with Christ. When
we lay Christ as the foundation, we are so happy that we
shout "Hallelujah!" We have no other foundation but Christ.
(*The Recovery of God's House and God's City*, p. 28)

Today's Reading

In Matthew 21:42 and 43 we see that Christ is the cornerstone of God's building....In Matthew 21:42 Christ is referred
to as the cornerstone, not as the foundation, because the
emphasis here is on the cornerstone that joins the two main
walls: the wall of the Jewish believers and the wall of the Gentile believers. (*The Conclusion of the New Testament*, p. 2817)

The topstone [in Zechariah 4:7] with shouts of "Grace, grace
to it!" signifies Christ, who is the grace as the stone, upon which
are the seven eyes of Jehovah, the sevenfold intensified Spirit of
God for the completion of the rebuilding of God's temple (3:9; 4:7-
10; Rev. 5:6). To bring forth the topstone is to complete the building. This topstone is a type of Christ....The topstone is...the
Christ who is the grace from God to us to be the covering of God's
building. (*Life-study of Zechariah*, pp. 30-31)

[In 1 Corinthians 3:12] gold, silver, and precious stones signify the various experiences of Christ in the virtues and attributes of the Triune God. It is with these that the apostles and
all spiritual believers build the church on the unique foundation of Christ. Gold may signify the divine nature of the Father
with all its attributes, silver may signify the redeeming Christ
with all the virtues and attributes of His person and work, and

precious stones may signify the transforming work of the Spirit with all its attributes. All these precious materials are the products of our participation in and enjoyment of Christ in our spirit through the Holy Spirit. Only these are good for God's building. (1 Cor. 3:12, footnote 2)

Christ became wisdom to us from God as three vital things in God's salvation: (1) righteousness (for our past), by which we have been justified by God, that we might be reborn in our spirit to receive the divine life (Rom. 5:18); (2) sanctification (for our present), by which we are being sanctified in our soul, that is, transformed in our mind, emotion, and will, with His divine life (Rom. 6:19, 22); and (3) redemption (for our future), that is, the redemption of our body (Rom. 8:23), by which we will be transfigured in our body with His divine life to have His glorious likeness (Phil. 3:21). (1 Cor. 1:30, footnote 2)

Paul lived a crucified life continually, a life under the cross, just as Christ did in His human living. Through such a life the resurrection power of Christ is experienced and expressed. The mold of Christ's death refers to Christ's experience of continually putting to death His human life that He might live by the life of God (John 6:57). Our life should be conformed to such a mold by our dying to our human life to live the divine life. Being conformed to the death of Christ is the condition for knowing and experiencing Him, the power of His resurrection, and the fellowship of His sufferings. (Phil. 3:10, footnote 4)

To experience Christ we need faith and love (1 Tim. 1:14). Faith enables us to apprehend Christ, and love enables us to enjoy Him. Neither faith nor love are ours; they are His. His faith becomes our faith, by which we believe in Him, and His love becomes our love, by which we love Him. When we are rooted and grounded in His love, we grow and are built up in His life. (Eph. 3:17, footnote 4)

Further Reading: The Recovery of Christ as Everything in the Church, chs. 1, 3-4

Enlightenment and inspiration: _____

_____

_____

_____

Hymns, #1252

1   Down in Babylon, in captivity,
    Oh, the Lord has stirred our spirit up!
  Scattered everywhere, without unity,
    Oh, the Lord has stirred our spirit up!
     Stirred up! Stirred up!
     Oh, the Lord has stirred our spirit up!

2   Up from Babylon, where the sects abound,
    From division we must all rise up!
  Brothers, Babylon's not the proper ground;
    From division we must all rise up!
     Rise up! Rise up!
     From division we must all rise up!

3   To Jerusalem, from captivity,
    God is with us, let us all go up!
  To the one unique ground of unity,
    God is with us, let us all go up!
     Go up! Go up!
     God is with us, let us all go up!

4   Platters full of Christ, bowls with Spirit filled —
    All the vessels of the Lord bring up!
  Bring them to the church as the Lord has willed —
    All the vessels of the Lord bring up
     Bring up! Bring up!
     All the vessels of the Lord bring up!

5   In Jerusalem, chosen of the Lord,
    Now the temple of the Lord build up!
  Serve with all the saints, share in one accord,
    Now the temple of the Lord build up!
     Build up! Build up!
     Now the temple of the Lord build up!

Composition for prophecy with main point and sub-points: _____

_____
_____
_____
_____
_____
_____
_____
_____
_____
_____
_____
_____
_____
_____
_____
_____
_____
_____
_____
_____
_____
_____
_____
_____
_____
_____
_____
_____
_____
_____
_____
_____
_____

Christic as the Stone
with the Seven Eyes of Jehovah
for God's Building

Scripture Reading: Zech. 3:9; 4:7-10; Rev. 5:6; Matt. 16:18

Day 1   I. **God's building is the mingling of God with man, the corporate expression of the Triune God, and the enlargement of God; the building of God is the Triune God as life being wrought into us so that we may become His corporate expression, the enlargement and expansion of God (John 3:29a, 30a; 14:20; 17:22; 1 John 4:15; Eph. 3:17a, 19b, 21; 1 Tim. 3:15-16).**

II. **In God's building Christ is everything (Matt. 16:18; 1 Pet. 2:4; 1 Cor. 3:11; Eph. 2:20):**

A. In God's building Christ is the rock, the Rock of Ages (Matt. 16:18):

1. This rock is Christ as the embodiment of the Triune God and as the consummation of the Triune God after the steps of His process (Col. 2:9; John 1:14; 20:22; 1 Cor. 15:45b).

2. The rock for the building of the temple of God is the processed Triune God (Matt. 16:18; 28:19).

B. Christ is the living stone for God's building (1 Pet. 2:4):

1. A living stone is one that not only possesses life but also grows in life; this is Christ for God's building (vv. 4-5; Col. 2:19).

2. After receiving Christ as the seed of life, we need to grow in order to experience Him as the stone living in us; in this way He makes us living stones, transformed with His stone nature so that we may be built together with others as a spiritual house (1 Pet. 1:23; 2:2-5; Eph. 2:22).

C. As the Christ and the Son of the living God, the Lord Jesus Christ, who is the all-inclusive One, is the unique foundation laid by God for His building; He is the unique One to be the unique foundation of the divine building (Matt. 16:16; 1 Cor. 3:11; Isa. 28:16).

Day 2   D. In God's building Christ is the cornerstone (Eph. 2:20):

1. As the cornerstone, Christ joins together the two walls, one wall being the Jewish believers, and the other, the Gentile believers (vv. 11-14).

2. Whether we are Jews or Gentiles, we have been saved in order to be joined in Christ for God's building (vv. 21-22).

III. **For God's building, the temple, Christ is the stone with seven eyes (Zech. 3:9; 4:7-10; Eph. 2:21; 1 Cor. 3:16-17):**

A. The stone set before Joshua in Zechariah 3:9 typifies Christ as the stone for God's building (Psa. 118:22; Matt. 21:42).

B. Jehovah's engraving of the stone indicates that God will work on Christ as the stone for the accomplishing of God's redemption, salvation, and building (Zech. 3:9):

1. To engrave is to cut; when Christ was dying on the cross, He was engraved, cut, by God.

2. This indicates that the Christ on whom God has worked will remove the sin of the land of Israel in one day, the day of His crucifixion; through His death on the cross, Christ, the Lamb of God, took away the sin of the world (1 Pet. 2:24; John 1:29).

C. The seven eyes of the stone (Christ) are the seven eyes of Jehovah and the seven eyes of the Lamb, Christ, which are the seven Spirits of God, the sevenfold intensified Spirit (Zech. 4:10; Rev. 5:6):

1. "These seven" in Zechariah 4:10, which are the seven eyes on the stone in 3:9, are the seven eyes of Jehovah and also the seven eyes of the Lamb (Rev. 1:4; 3:1; 5:6).

    2. The stone, Jehovah, and the Lamb are one:

      a. Christ is the redeeming Lamb and the building stone, and He is also Jehovah; Christ is the Lamb-stone—the Lamb for redemption and the stone for building (John 1:29; Matt. 21:42; Zech. 2:8, 11).

Day 3

      b. The seven eyes of Christ are the seven Spirits of God, indicating that Christ and the Holy Spirit, although distinct, are not separate; the Holy Spirit is essentially one with Christ (Rev. 5:6; Rom. 8:9-10; 2 Cor. 3:17).

      c. The seven eyes combine Jehovah, the Lamb, and the stone; the Lamb is the stone, and the stone is Jehovah (Zech. 3:9; 4:10; Rev. 5:6).

    3. The fact that Christ, the Lamb of God, is the building stone with seven eyes reveals that the seven eyes of Christ are for God's building (John 1:29; Zech. 3:9; Rev. 5:6).

    4. Christ is the building stone with seven eyes, with the seven Spirits to transfuse Himself into us in order to transform us into precious materials for God's building (Zech. 3:9; 1 Cor. 3:12a; Rev. 3:1):

Day 4

      a. The seven eyes of Christ as the Lamb and as the stone, which are the seven Spirits of God, are Christ's expression in God's move for God's building (1:4; 3:1).

      b. As the Lord looks at us, His seven eyes transfuse Himself into us; He transmits His inner being into us through His eyes (5:6).

IV. For the completion of God's building Christ is the topstone of grace (Zech. 4:7):

    A. In God's building Christ is the foundation stone to uphold the building, the cornerstone to join together the Gentile and Jewish members of His Body, and the topstone to consummate everything in God's building (Isa. 28:16; 1 Cor. 3:11; Eph. 2:20; 1 Pet. 2:6; Zech. 4:7).

B. The topstone with shouts of "Grace, grace to it" signifies Christ, who is the grace as the stone, upon which are the seven eyes of Jehovah, for the completion of the rebuilding of God's temple (3:9; 4:7-10; Rev. 5:6):

1. To bring forth the topstone is to complete the building; this topstone is a type of Christ (Zech. 4:7).

2. The shouts of "Grace, grace to it" indicate that the topstone itself is grace; the topstone is grace from God to us, and this grace is Christ (v. 7; John 1:14, 16; 2 Cor. 13:14).

3. The topstone is the Christ who is grace from God to us to be the covering of God's building (Zech. 4:7).

Day 5 V. **Through the transfusing of the sevenfold intensified Spirit, the seven eyes of Christ as the engraved stone, we become the same as Christ in life, nature, and expression for God's building (Eph. 3:19b, 21):**

A. The high peak of the divine revelation is that God became man so that man may become God in life and nature but not in the Godhead to produce and build up the organic Body of Christ as the corporate expression of the Triune God (John 1:12-14; 1 John 3:1-2; Rom. 8:3; 12:4-5).

B. The Scriptures reveal that God's intention is to make His chosen, redeemed, and regenerated people the reproduction of Christ for the temple of God—the Body of Christ—as the corporate expression of the Triune God (John 1:12-14; 12:24; Rom. 1:3-4; 8:3, 29; 12:4-5):

1. In Song of Songs we see that, as the reproduction of Christ, the loving seekers of the Lord become the sanctuary of God and a corporate Shulammite (6:4, 13).

Day 6 2. According to the Gospel of John, Christ has

a reproduction for God's building (12:24; 2:19-22; 14:2):

  a. As a grain of wheat, the Lord Jesus fell into the ground and died in order to produce many grains in resurrection as His reproduction (12:24; Eph. 2:6).

  b. In Christ's resurrection we are His reproduction; in His resurrection He imparted the divine life into us, making us the same as He is in life and nature to be His reproduction for God's building, the temple of God (John 2:19-22; 12:24; 1 Pet. 1:3; 1 Cor. 3:16-17).

3. The deep thought in Romans is that God became man so that, in God's complete salvation, sinners may be redeemed, regenerated, sanctified, renewed, transformed, conformed, and glorified to become the sons of God, who are the same as God in life and nature, to be the members of the Body of Christ (8:3; 1:3-4; 3:24; 5:10; 8:14, 29-30; 12:4-5).

4. The book of Hebrews reveals that through the function of the law of life, we become the reproduction of Christ as the firstborn Son of God to be the church, which is a living composition of the many sons of God (1:6; 2:10-12).

5. In Revelation the living person of Jesus is the expression and testimony of God, and the church is the testimony of Jesus, the corporate expression of Christ; as such, the church, the enlarged Christ, is the reproduction of the testimony and expression of God in Christ, consummating in the New Jerusalem as the ultimate and consummate corporate expression of the Triune God in the new heaven and new earth (1:2, 5, 9, 12, 20; 21:2, 10-11).

Morning Nourishment

1 Cor. For another foundation no one is able to lay be-
3:11 sides that which is laid, which is Jesus Christ.
1 Pet. Coming to Him, a living stone, rejected by men but
2:4-5 with God chosen *and* precious, you yourselves also, as
living stones, are being built up as a spiritual house...

Building is the enlargement of God to express God in a corporate way. We have seen that life is God Himself wrought into our being. If the Triune God has truly been wrought into us, the issue will be an enlargement and an expansion of God.

Thus, when we speak of the building of God, we mean that the Triune God as life is being wrought into us continually and that under His transfusion and infusion we are becoming His one expression. This expression is His enlargement and expansion. May this thought be written on our heart. (*Life-study of John*, pp. 5-6)

Today's Reading

In God's building there is the need for a rock, and this rock is Christ (Matt. 16:18)....God's building is built absolutely on this rock, which is the Rock of Ages. This rock is Christ as the embodiment of the Triune God (Col. 2:9) and as the consummation of the Triune God after the steps of His process. Therefore, the rock for the building of God's house is the consummated Triune God.

Christ is also the stone, the living stone, for God's building. First Peter 2:4 speaks of Christ as a living stone: "Coming to Him, a living stone...." A living stone is one that not only possesses life but also grows in life. This is Christ for God's building. As life to us, Christ is the seed. For God's building, He is the stone. After receiving Him as the seed of life, we need to grow that we may experience Him as the stone living in us. In this way He makes us also living stones, transformed with His stone nature so that we may be built together with others a spiritual house upon Him as both the foundation and the cornerstone (Isa. 28:16).

In Christ and through Christ we also become living stones to be built up a spiritual house (1 Pet. 2:5). We, the believers in Christ, are living stones, like Christ, through regeneration and transformation. We were created of clay (Rom. 9:21). But at regeneration we received the seed of the divine life, which by its growth in us transforms us into living stones. At Peter's conversion the Lord gave him a new name—Peter, a stone (John 1:42). When Peter received the revelation concerning Christ, the Lord revealed further that He was also the rock (Matt. 16:16-18). Peter realized by these two incidents that both Christ and His believers are stones for God's building. In actuality we become stones through the process of transformation. In this process our natural life is replaced by Christ, and Christ becomes us, thereby making us the precious materials for God's building. Today we are undergoing the process of transformation so that Christ, the living stone, may be constituted into us to make us living stones for God's building.

The spiritual house into which we are being built is God's building. Eventually this building will consummate in the New Jerusalem. In the New Jerusalem there will not be any clay, for all the clay will have been transformed into precious stone. This indicates that the New Jerusalem is built with precious stones. We are becoming the precious stones that will be built up into the New Jerusalem. This process takes place as we daily contact Christ, the living stone for God's building, and are transformed.

In God's building Christ is the unique foundation. "Another foundation no one is able to lay besides that which is laid, which is Jesus Christ" (1 Cor. 3:11). As the Christ and the Son of the living God, the Lord Jesus Christ is the unique foundation laid by God for His building. No one can lay any other foundation. Christ is the all-inclusive One. Nothing and no one can compare with Him. Nothing and no one, other than He, are qualified to be the foundation of the divine building in the universe according to God's eternal economy. He is the unique One to be the unique foundation of this divine building. (*The Conclusion of the New Testament,* pp. 638-639)

Further Reading: Life-study of John, msg. 1; *The Vision of God's Building,* ch. 11

Enlightenment and inspiration: _____

_____

_____

_____

Morning Nourishment

Eph. Being built upon the foundation of the apostles and
2:20 prophets, Christ Jesus Himself being the cornerstone.
Zech. For here is the stone that I have set before Joshua—
3:9 upon one stone are seven eyes. I will engrave its
engraving, declares Jehovah of hosts, and I will
remove the iniquity of that land in one day.

Ephesians 2:20 says that in God's building Christ is the cornerstone. In this verse Christ is referred to as the cornerstone, not as the foundation, because the main concern here is the cornerstone that joins the two main walls: the wall of the Jewish believers and the wall of the Gentile believers. When the Jewish builders rejected Christ, they rejected Him as the cornerstone (Acts 4:11; 1 Pet. 2:7), which joins the Gentiles to them for the building of God's house.

God's intention in saving us is not to bring us into the heavens; rather, it is to join us to the Jews so that He may have His building. Many unbelieving Jews reject the Lord Jesus because they do not want to be joined to the Gentiles. As long as a Jew does not believe in Christ, he may be separated from the Gentiles. But as soon as a Jew believes in Him, he is joined by Christ, the cornerstone, to the Gentile believers. Whether we are Jews or Gentiles, we have been saved in order to be joined in Christ for God's building. (*The Conclusion of the New Testament,* pp. 639-640)

Today's Reading

It is crucial for us to see that God's building in the New Testament age is altogether with Christ. In this building Christ is everything. This is why we should learn to minister nothing other than Christ to the believers. For God's building we need Christ as everything to us. (*The Conclusion of the New Testament,* p. 640)

[In Zechariah 3:9] this stone (Zerubbabel) set before Joshua also typifies Christ (Isa. 28:16; Matt. 21:42). Zerubbabel was a stone set before Joshua to carry out God's economy.

Upon this one stone (Christ) are seven eyes (Zech. 3:9a; 4:10).

These seven eyes signify the sevenfold intensified Spirit (Rev. 5:6). Christ is the stone with the seven Spirits as His eyes.

Jehovah will engrave the engraving of the stone (Zech. 3:9b). This indicates that God will work on Christ as the stone for God's redemption, salvation, and building. To engrave is to cut. When Christ was on the cross, He was engraved, cut, by God.

Furthermore, Jehovah will remove the iniquity of that land in one day (v. 9c). This indicates that the Christ on whom God has worked will redeem the sin of the land of Israel in one day, the day of His crucifixion (1 Pet. 2:24). Through His death on the cross, Christ the Lamb of God took away the sin of the world (John 1:29). (*Life-study of Zechariah,* pp. 23-24)

[In Zechariah 4:10] "these seven," which are the eyes of Jehovah, are the seven eyes on the stone in 3:9. The seven eyes of the stone are the seven eyes of Jehovah and also the seven eyes of the Lamb, Christ (Rev. 5:6). Thus, the stone, Jehovah, and the Lamb are one. Christ is the redeeming Lamb and the building stone, and He is also Jehovah. (Zech. 4:10, footnote 1)

We know that a stone is material for God's building. But before the Lord can build us up, He must get rid of our iniquity. Therefore, the stone becomes a lamb. This is why the seven eyes on the stone are the seven eyes of the Lamb [Rev. 5:6]. On the cross God engraved Christ to remove the iniquity of God's people. This is not only for redemption but for the building of God. When the Lord Jesus was surrounded by His opposers, He indicated that He Himself is a stone. He said that the stone which the builders rejected had become the head of the corner (Matt. 21:42). This is the "Lamb-stone." He is both the Lamb and the stone: the Lamb is for our redemption, and the stone is for God's building. Redemption is for building. So eventually He is the Lamb-stone—the Lamb-stone with seven eyes. (*The Wonderful Christ in the Canon of the New Testament,* p. 190)

Further Reading: The Conclusion of the New Testament, msg. 59; *Life-study of Revelation,* msgs. 22, 33

Enlightenment and inspiration: _____

_____

_____

_____

Morning Nourishment

**Zech. ...These seven rejoice when they see the plummet
4:10 in the hand of Zerubbabel; they are the eyes of
Jehovah running to and fro on the whole earth.**

**Rev. And I saw in the midst of the throne...a Lamb
5:6 standing as having *just* been slain, having seven
horns and seven eyes, which are the seven Spirits
of God sent forth into all the earth.**

The seven eyes of Christ are the seven Spirits of God (see footnotes 6[5] in Rev. 5 and 4[5] in Rev. 1), indicating that Christ and the Holy Spirit, although distinct, are not separate. Just as a person's eyes are essentially one with the person, so the Holy Spirit is essentially one with Christ (Rom. 8:9-10; 2 Cor. 3:17). The function of Christ's seven eyes is to observe and search in order to execute God's judgment on the universe and to transfuse and infuse all that God is into His chosen people. In His resurrection Christ, as the last Adam, became the life-giving Spirit (1 Cor. 15:45b; John 6:63a; 2 Cor. 3:6b), who is also the sevenfold intensified Spirit. This Spirit is the Spirit of life (Rom. 8:2). Hence, the function of the seven Spirits is to impart the divine life into God's people for the building up of God's eternal habitation, the New Jerusalem. (Zech. 4:10, footnote 1)

Today's Reading

In Revelation 4 and 5 we have a further development of the seven lamps. According to 4:5, the seven lamps of the lampstand are seven lamps of fire burning before the throne of God. The seven lamps on the lampstand were for enlightening, but the seven lamps before the throne of God are both for enlightening and for the carrying out of God's administrative government. Revelation 5:6 indicates that the seven lamps burning before the throne are also the seven eyes of the Lamb. Thus, the seven eyes are the seven eyes of the stone, the seven eyes of the Lord, and the seven eyes of the Lamb. These seven eyes combine the stone, the Lord, and the Lamb. This indicates that the Lamb is the stone and that the stone is the Lord. Moreover, 5:6 reveals that the seven eyes of the Lamb are the seven Spirits of God. On the one hand, there is a line containing six items: the lampstand, the stone, Jehovah, the Lamb, the throne of God, and God. On the other hand, there is another line with three items: the seven lamps, the seven eyes, and the seven Spirits. (*Life-study of Revelation,* p. 778)

The seven lamps in Zechariah 4 are, without a doubt, the seven eyes of God. These seven eyes cannot be another seven eyes in addition to the seven eyes in chapter 3. The seven eyes in chapter 3 are the seven eyes on the stone, and the seven eyes in chapter 4 are the seven eyes of Jehovah. Therefore, this implies that the seven eyes of Jehovah are upon the stone. Who is the stone? The stone is Jehovah! The stone is Jesus, and the name Jesus means "Jehovah the Savior." Thus, the seven eyes on the stone are the seven eyes of Jehovah because the stone is Jehovah. The stone is Jesus, who is Jehovah—the redeeming Jehovah, Jehovah who removes our iniquities, Jehovah as our Savior, and Jehovah as the Lamb of God. Therefore, His seven eyes are God's seven eyes....In brief, the seven eyes are the seven Spirits of God for His building. (*The Revelation of the Mystery,* pp. 32-33)

The stone that was rejected by the builders and that became the cornerstone (Matt. 21:42; Acts 4:11) is the very stone with the seven eyes in Zechariah 3:9....Christ died as the Lamb, but in resurrection God made Him the cornerstone. On this stone there are seven eyes shining and burning to carry out God's economy. Because in Zechariah these seven eyes are on the stone and in Revelation they are on the Lamb, we may say that Christ, the Lamb and the stone, is the Lamb-stone for God's building. The fact that Christ, the Lamb of God, is the building stone with seven eyes reveals that the seven eyes of Christ are for God's building. Our Christ is the building stone with seven eyes, with the seven Spirits to infuse Himself into us in order to transform us into precious materials for God's building. (*The Conclusion of the New Testament,* p. 487)

Further Reading: The Revelation of the Mystery, ch. 4; *Life-study of Revelation,* msg. 68

Enlightenment and inspiration: _____

_____

_____

_____

Morning Nourishment

John And the Word became flesh and tabernacled among
1:14 us (and we beheld His glory, glory as of the only Begotten from the Father), full of grace and reality.
16 For of His fullness we have all received, and grace
upon grace.
2 Cor. The grace of the Lord Jesus Christ and the love of God
13:14 and the fellowship of the Holy Spirit be with you all.

The Son is the embodiment of the Father, and the Spirit is the expression of the Son. The seven eyes of Christ, the seven Spirits of God, are Christ's expression in a judging way in God's move for God's building. Even now, Christ's burning eyes are flaming over us to enlighten, search, refine, and judge us, not that we might be condemned, but that we might be purged, transformed, and conformed to His image for God's building. (*Life-study of Revelation*, pp. 228-229)

Today's Reading

The seven eyes of the Lamb are for transfusing and infusing. After the seven Spirits of God as the seven lamps of fire burn within us, in our experience they become seven eyes....If a person closes his eyes, we cannot see what is lovely in him. A person's loveliness is in his eyes. After we experience the burning, judging, and purifying, the burning lamps of fire become the lovely eyes. We may wonder whether these seven eyes are fearful or lovely.... Whether the Lord's eyes are fearful or lovely depends not on Him but on us. If we live properly as children of God, His eyes will be lovely, but if we are disobedient, His eyes will be fearful. Regardless of whether His transfusion is that of love or of fear, as He looks at us with His eyes, God is transfused into us.

Whenever the Lord looks at us, we receive a precious infusion. When one person looks at another person, he transfuses his feeling into that person. A person's eyes are the expression of his inner being. To transfuse is to transmit a person's inner being into the one whom he is looking at (cf. 2 Cor. 2:10). The seven Spirits are the seven eyes by which Christ expresses Him-self. As the Lord looks at us, His seven eyes transfuse Himself into us. Whenever the Lord looks at us with His eyes, we can understand if He is happy or unhappy. There is no need for Him to say anything. By looking at us, He transfuses all that He is into our being. His seven eyes are gazing at us to infuse God into us. (*The Conclusion of the New Testament*, pp. 4243-4244)

In the fourth vision [in Zechariah] Christ is unveiled as the topstone of grace (4:7). As indicated in 3:9, upon this stone are seven eyes, signifying the seven Spirits, that is, the sevenfold intensified Spirit. Christ is therefore the topstone of grace to con-summate God's building with the sevenfold intensified Spirit.

The topstone with shouts of "Grace, grace to it!" signifies Christ, who is the grace as the stone, upon which are the seven eyes of Jehovah, the sevenfold intensified Spirit of God for the completion of the rebuilding of God's temple (3:9; 4:7-10; Rev. 5:6). To bring forth the topstone is to complete the building. This topstone is a type of Christ. For God's building Christ is a stone in three aspects. Christ is the foundation stone to uphold God's building (Isa. 28:16; 1 Cor. 3:11), the cornerstone to join together the Gentile and Jewish members of His Body (Eph. 2:20; 1 Pet. 2:6), and the topstone to consummate everything of God's building.

The shouts of "Grace, grace to it!" indicate that the topstone itself is grace. The topstone is grace from God to us, and this grace is Christ...(John 1:14). This reveals that in His incarnation Christ brought God to us first as grace and then as reality. Grace is God in the Son as our enjoyment; reality is God realized by us in the Son. When God is enjoyed by us, we have grace. When God is real-ized by us, we have reality. Both grace and reality are Christ. The topstone is therefore the Christ who is the grace from God to us to be the covering of God's building. (*Life-study of Zechariah*, pp. 94, 30-31)

Further Reading: Life-study of Zechariah, msg. 5; The Conclusion of the New Testament, msg. 416

Enlightenment and inspiration: _____

_____

_____

_____

Morning Nourishment

1 John Beloved, now we are children of God, and it has not
3:2   yet been manifested what we will be. We know that
        if He is manifested, we will be like Him because we
        will see Him even as He is.

S.S.   You are as beautiful, my love, as Tirzah, as lovely as
6:4   Jerusalem, as terrible as an army with banners.

13   Return, return, O Shulammite; return, return, that
        we may gaze at you. Why should you gaze at the
        Shulammite, as upon the dance of two camps?

We need to realize that Satan hates the high peak of the divine
revelation concerning the ultimate goal of God's economy. He hates
this one main point—that God became a man so that man may
become God in life and in nature but not in the Godhead to
produce the organic Body of Christ for the fulfillment of God's
economy to close this age and to bring Christ back to set up His
kingdom. This is why we need prayer for fighting the spiritual
warfare....God purposely in His incarnation became a man that
man may become God in life and nature but not in the Godhead
for the producing of the organic Body of Christ to fulfill God's
economy to close this age and to bring Christ back with His kingdom. (*Crystallization-study of the Epistle to the Romans,* p. 159)

Today's Reading

On the one hand, we are God's household as members of
God's house, God's family; on the other hand, we are God's dwelling place on earth, and we have God dwelling in our spirit. God
obtains a dwelling place for His rest within us. We must realize
that if there were not a group of people who allowed God to work
Himself into them, God would become homeless.

God works Himself into us that we may have an organic union
with the Divine Trinity in Christ to become the members of Christ
that constitute His Body as the corporate expression of the Triune
God in Christ....In our organic union with the Divine Trinity we
become the members of Christ; that is, we become His bone and
His flesh (Eph. 5:30-32). Collectively, as members of Christ we are

constituted into one Body as a corporate expression of the Triune God in Christ. (*The Revelation and Vision of God,* pp. 101-103)

Through her living in Christ's ascension as the new creation in resurrection, the lover of Christ becomes mature in the riches of the life of Christ so that she becomes not only a garden to Christ but also the sanctuary of God, signified by Tirzah, and its safeguard, signified by Jerusalem. To be mature in the life of Christ is a great thing. The seeker is likened to two buildings. One is the palace of the king. The other is the city surrounding the palace as its safeguard. A garden cannot be compared with a palace and a city. A garden is just a visiting place for the king, but it is not the dwelling place where the king lives or the city that safeguards the king's palace....To become a garden to Christ is to be flourishing in the element of Christ's life with its unsearchable riches; to become the sanctuary of God is to be built up (related to the building of the Body of Christ) in the growth with the life of Christ with its unsearchable riches (Eph. 4:15-16). In the Old Testament the building of God is typified by Tirzah and Jerusalem; in the New Testament this building is the organic Body of Christ. The organic Body of Christ is also Christ's wife (Eph. 5:25-32). Furthermore, the organic Body of Christ consummates, completes, the building of the New Jerusalem. (*Crystallization-study of Song of Songs,* pp. 95-96)

In Song of Songs the seeker passes through a process to become the Shulammite, the duplication of Solomon and a figure of the New Jerusalem (6:13, 4)....The lover of Christ becomes the same as He is in life, nature, and image to match Him (2 Cor. 3:18; Rom. 8:29) for their marriage. The lover of Solomon, having passed through various stages of transformation, has become Solomon's duplication. The New Jerusalem will be a corporate Shulammite, including all of God's chosen and redeemed people. (*The Conclusion of the New Testament,* p. 4372)

Further Reading: The Building of God, chs. 1, 3-4; *The Conclusion of the New Testament,* msg. 428

Enlightenment and inspiration: _____

_____

_____

_____

Morning Nourishment

John In My Father's house are many abodes; if *it were* not so, I
14:2 would have told you; for I go to prepare a place for you.
Rev. And I saw the holy city, New Jerusalem, coming
21:2-3 down out of heaven from God, prepared as a bride
       adorned for her husband. And I heard a loud voice
       out of the throne, saying, Behold, the tabernacle of
       God is with men, and He will tabernacle with them...

In Christ's resurrection we are His reproduction. Concerning
this, Peter says, "The God and Father of our Lord Jesus Christ...
has regenerated us unto a living hope through the resurrection of
Jesus Christ from the dead" (1 Pet. 1:3)...We [His believers] were
resurrected with Him (Eph. 2:6). In His resurrection Christ imparted the divine life into us and made us the same as He is in life
and nature to be His reproduction. He was a grain of wheat falling
into the ground to die. When He grew up in resurrection, He produced many grains. The many grains are His reproduction, His
multiplication, and this reproduction is His propagation. Through
His death and resurrection He has been multiplied and propa-
gated. This propagation is for the producing of the church. Through
His death and resurrection He has produced the church as His reproduction. (*The Conclusion of the New Testament,* p. 323)

Today's Reading

In the Lord's last words to the believers in John 14—16, there
are three concrete, corporate expressions of...glory: the Father's
house (the church) in 14:2, the branches of the vine (the constitu-
ents of the Body of Christ) in 15:1-5, and a newborn corporate man
(the new man) in 16:21. All three denote the church, showing
that the church is the glorious increase produced by the glorious
Christ through His death and resurrection. In this glorious increase, Christ, the Son of God, is glorified, causing God the Father also
to be glorified in Christ's glorification, that is, to be fully expressed
through the church (Eph. 3:19-21). (John 12:24, footnote 2)

Christ, equal to *Messiah* in Hebrew, means *the anointed One*
(John 1:41; Dan. 9:26). [Romans] explains how the individual

Christ revealed in the four Gospels could become the corporate Christ revealed in Acts, collectively composed of Himself with all the believers. By means of the facts in the Scriptures and the experience in the Holy Spirit, Paul shows us that God's New Testament economy is to make sinners sons of God and members of Christ to constitute the Body of Christ to express Him. This book offers a full definition of this, God's goal, unfolding a general sketch and details of both the Christian life and the church life. (Rom. 1:1, footnote 3)

Praise the Lord that we have had a new birth, a divine birth. In this new birth there are no weak points. There is only the divine life with the divine nature and the divine law, which shapes us and conforms us to the image of Christ. However, this shaping requires the growth in life; for the law of life only functions as life grows. The law of life does not regulate us from sin, because it is not in the realm of sin; it is in the realm of the divine life where there is no sin, world, flesh, or self. As life grows, its law works, not mainly to regulate or correct us, but to shape us, to conform us to the image of the firstborn Son of God. Eventually, through the function of the law of life, we all shall become the mature sons of God, and God will have His universal, corporate expression. (*Life-study of Hebrews,* pp. 771-772)

God's goal in His creation of man was to have a corporate expression of Himself. According to this goal, man was made in the image of God in order to be His testimony (Gen. 1:26)…. Because Adam failed God in this respect, Jesus came as the second man (1 Cor. 15:47b) to take the position and function of Adam. Thus, the living person of Jesus is the expression, image, and testimony of God (Col. 1:15). In the same way, the church today is the testimony of Jesus, that is, His expression. In the first chapter of the Bible, man is in the image of God to express God, and in the last two chapters of the Bible there is a building, the New Jerusalem, to express God. (*The Testimony of Jesus,* p. 61)

Further Reading: The Conclusion of the New Testament, msgs. 30, 210; *Life-study of Romans,* msg. 53

Enlightenment and inspiration: _____

_____

_____

_____

Hymns, #834

1   The chief Cornerstone Thou art, Lord,
    Jewish builders did despise;
  God by resurrection placed Thee,
    Thou art precious in His eyes.
  Through Thee we receive salvation,
    And, together built by Thee,
  Jews and Gentiles are Thy dwelling,
    One new man, in harmony.

2   Thou too art the smitten Rock, Lord,
    That man's thirst by Thee be filled,
  That frail man may stand upon Thee,
    But e'en more, God's house to build.
  The Foundation Stone in Zion,
    Tested and secure, Thou art;
  And the Rock, the Church supporting,
    Her foundation to impart.

3   On Thyself the Church is builded,
    And though many storms assail,
  Still it stands erect, for 'gainst it
    Gates of hell cannot prevail.
  Thine authority possessing,
    It doth bind and loose in Thee,
  Bringing men into Thy kingdom,
    Satan's captives setting free.

4   Living Stone of life art Thou, Lord,
    Precious, chosen thus to be;
  Living stones Thou too hast made us,
    One in character with Thee.
  Built together as a temple
    That our God may dwell therein,
  Thus we are a holy priesthood,
    Offering sacrifice to Him.

7   Thou art God, yet flesh becamest,
    God with man in Thee doth dwell;
  Thou, the Temple for His glory,
    God in Thee Himself doth tell.
  Thus the Church too is the mingling
    Into one of God and man;
  So it is with every member
    For the building of God's plan.

8   Thou, the everlasting Dwelling,
      In all ages art our home;
    We in Thee enjoy protection,
      Living in Thyself alone.
    Thou our Sanctuary art, Lord,
      We and God abide in Thee;
    Thou, God's presence art within us,
      Where we worship ceaselessly.

9   Cornerstone, Foundation, Topstone,
      Rock, and Church, and Living Stone,
    Dwelling-place, and Sanctuary,
      Builder too art Thou, we own.
    Praise we give for what Thou art, Lord,
      As Thy wondrousness we see!
    Grant that we may be built up, Lord,
      As the living stones in Thee.

Composition for prophecy with main point and sub-points: _____

_____

_____

_____

_____

_____

_____

_____

_____

_____

_____

_____

_____

_____

_____

_____

_____

_____

_____

_____

_____

The Vision of the Golden Lampstand and the Two Olive Trees

Scripture Reading: Zech. 4

Day 1   I. **We need to have a spirit of wisdom and revelation to see a vision of the golden lampstand, which was designed by God Himself and portrays the goal of His eternal economy (Eph. 1:17; Zech. 4:1-5; Rev. 1:2, 9-12):**
   A. The golden lampstand signifies the Triune God:
      1. The pure gold substance signifies God the Father in His divine nature (Exo. 25:31).
      2. The stand signifies God the Son as the image and embodiment of God the Father (2 Cor. 4:4b; Col. 1:15; 2:9).
      3. The lamps signify God the Spirit as the seven Spirits of God for the expression of the Father in the Son (Exo. 25:37; Rev. 4:5).
   B. The lampstand in Exodus, the lampstand in Zechariah, and the lampstands in Revelation are three stages of the truth concerning the lampstand:
Day 2   1. The lampstand in the tabernacle in Exodus 25:31-40 signifies Christ Himself as the embodiment of the Triune God, the lampstand in Zechariah 4:2-10 signifies the sevenfold intensified life-giving Spirit as the reality of Christ, and the lampstands in Revelation 1:12 and 20 signify the churches as the reproduction of Christ and the reprint of the Spirit.
      2. Thus, the church is the reprint of the Spirit, who is the reality of Christ, who is the embodiment of God.
   II. **Zechariah 4 tells us that when Zechariah saw the lampstand, he asked the angel what this was; then the angel answered, "This is the word of Jehovah to Zerubbabel, saying, Not by might nor by power, but by My Spirit,**

says Jehovah of hosts" (v. 6):

A. The Lord told Zechariah that the lampstand was His Spirit; thus, the lampstand first signifies Christ, then the Spirit, and ultimately the church; this indicates that the very Christ is the Spirit and that the Spirit with the very Christ produces the churches.

B. The ultimate definition of the church is that the church is the reproduction of Christ and the reprint of the Spirit.

C. When we say that we are the church, we must realize that we have to be fully in the Spirit; if we all are in the Spirit, we are the church in reality (Eph. 4:4; Gal. 5:16, 22-23, 25; 1 Cor. 12:7; Eph. 5:18; Zech. 4:6).

D. Since we are standing as the church in our locality, we must be in the Spirit, because the church is the reproduction of Christ and the reprint of the Spirit.

E. Christ has been regenerated into our being (John 1:12-13; 3:6b), and we are being fully transformed into His being (2 Cor. 3:18); as the Spirit, He is the lampstand, and the church is also the lampstand; we have to see what the church is to such an extent; if we see this vision of the church, we will be afraid to exercise our flesh (Gal. 5:16).

Day 3

F. The Spirit is the ultimate consummation of the processed Triune God, and the church is the reprint of the Spirit, the corporate expression of the Triune God; based on this we may say, "No Spirit, no church. More Spirit, more church."

G. Our natural being has no share in the church, no part in the church, because the church is the reprint of the Spirit; the church as the lampstand is pure and without mixture.

H. We need a governing vision that terminates, kills, and annuls everything of our natural man; if this vision is shining so brightly within us, the Lord will have a way to speak to us in our daily life to terminate our natural man (cf. 2:20).

  I. The "good manners" for the church life are our reborn, indwelt spirit (John 3:6b; Rom. 8:16; 2 Tim. 4:22; 1 Cor. 6:17); in our spirit we have the reprint of the divine Spirit, which is the church in practicality.

Day 4   **III. The seven lamps of the lampstand (Zech. 4:2; Rev. 4:5) are the seven Spirits of God, the sevenfold intensified Spirit (1:4), as the seven eyes of Jehovah (Zech. 4:10), the seven eyes of the redeeming Lamb (Rev. 5:6), and the seven eyes of the building stone (Zech. 3:9) for the full expression of the Triune God:**

  A. The sevenfold intensified Spirit is the eyes of Christ as the redeeming Lamb and the building stone to observe and search us and to infuse and transfuse us with Christ's essence, riches, and burden for God's building (v. 9; 4:7; Rev. 1:14; 5:6).

  B. The seven eyes of the Lamb infuse us with Christ as the judicial Redeemer, and the seven eyes of the stone infuse us with Christ as the organic Savior for God's economical move on earth through His judicial redemption and by His organic salvation for the goal of His building (John 1:29; Acts 4:11-12; Rom. 5:10; 1 Cor. 3:12).

  C. Within us we have two lamps—the sevenfold intensified Spirit of God within our spirit (Prov. 20:27; Rev. 4:5; 1 Cor. 6:17):

    1. In order to be transformed, we must fully open to the Lord in prayer to allow the lamp of the Lord with the seven lamps of fire to search all the chambers of our soul, shining on and enlightening our inward parts to supply them with life (2:11a; Eph. 6:18).

    2. The one who experiences the greatest amount of transformation is the one who is fully open to the Lord.

  D. In His resurrection Christ, as the last Adam, became the life-giving Spirit (1 Cor. 15:45b; John

6:63a; 2 Cor. 3:6b), who is also the sevenfold intensified Spirit; this Spirit is the Spirit of life (Rom. 8:2); hence, the function of the seven Spirits is to impart the divine life into God's people for the building up of God's eternal habitation, the New Jerusalem.

Day 5   E. The seven Spirits are burning before the throne to carry out God's administration, to execute God's economy in the universe, by directing the world situation.

F. The sevenfold intensified Spirit is the seven lamps of fire to burn, enlighten, expose, judge, purify, and refine us to produce the golden lampstands for the fulfillment of God's New Testament economy (Rev. 4:5).

G. The seven Spirits, who are the lamps of fire in this age executing God's New Testament economy, will become the river of water saturating the holy city of God, the New Jerusalem (22:1-2).

H. By the operation of the sevenfold intensified Spirit within Christ's seeking believers, they are intensified to become the overcomers to build up the Body of Christ, which consummates the New Jerusalem.

Day 6 **IV. We need to see the vision of the two olive trees on the two sides of the lampstand (Zech. 4:11-14):**

A. The two olive trees signify Joshua the high priest and Zerubbabel the governor at the time, who were the two sons of oil, filled with the Spirit of Jehovah for the rebuilding of God's temple (vv. 3-6, 12-14):

1. The building up of God's dwelling place is a noble work to be done by all God's people (1 Cor. 3:10; Eph. 4:12, 16); however, the wisdom, understanding, knowledge, and skill for this work must be God Himself as the Spirit to us (Exo. 31:2-6; cf. Col. 1:28-29).

2. Only the Spirit of God can build His own

dwelling place through us (Zech. 4:6; Eph. 2:21-22; 1 Cor. 3:16-17; 6:19).

3. To bring forth the topstone is to complete the building; the shouts of "Grace, grace to it" indicate that the topstone itself is grace; the topstone typifies Christ, who is the grace from God to us to be the covering of God's building (Zech. 4:7; 1 Cor. 15:10; 2 Cor. 1:12; 12:7-9).

4. Christ is the foundation stone to uphold God's building (Isa. 28:16; 1 Cor. 3:11), the cornerstone to join together the Gentile and Jewish members of His Body (Eph. 2:20; 1 Pet. 2:6), and the topstone to consummate God's building.

B. The two sons of oil also typify the two witnesses, Moses and Elijah, in the last three and a half years of the present age, who will be witnesses of God in the great tribulation for the strengthening of God's peoples—the Israelites and the believers in Christ (Rev. 11:3-12; 12:17).

C. In principle, all the believers in Christ should be sons of fresh oil, those who are filled with the Spirit as the oil to flow out the Spirit into the lampstand for its shining testimony, the testimony of Jesus (cf. 1:2, 9; Psa. 92:10):

1. The church as the lampstand is the solid embodiment of the Triune God with the sevenfold intensified Spirit as the oil of God in His divine nature.

2. The oil itself is gold (Zech. 4:12), which means that the gold flows as oil; when more oil is added into the lampstand, that means more gold is added.

3. We need to pay the price to gain more gold, more of God in His divine nature (2 Pet. 1:4; Rev. 3:18; Zech. 4:12-14; Matt. 25:8-9).

4. As we apply this matter to our experience today, we see that the Spirit who flows out of

us is God, and God is gold; thus, when we minister Christ to others, supplying them with oil, we are actually supplying them with God; God is flowing out from us into them.

5. We all should be olive trees emptying God from ourselves into others; in this way oil will be provided to the needy by those who are olive trees out of which God is flowing (Rom. 11:17; Luke 10:34; cf. John 7:37-39).

Morning Nourishment

Zech.
4:2
And he said to me, What do you see? And I said, I see that there is a lampstand all of gold, with its bowl on top of it and its seven lamps upon it, with seven pipes for each of the lamps on top of it.

Rev.
4:5
And out of the throne come forth lightnings and voices and thunders. And *there were* seven lamps of fire burning before the throne, which are the seven Spirits of God.

Can you think of a picture that shows us that God is our life, that we are the living of God, that He lives within us, and that for us to live is God? There is such a picture!

A most comprehensive picture is the golden lampstand, which is first mentioned in Exodus 25. There it stood in the tabernacle as a testimony for God. Zechariah 4 is the second mention. There the lampstand represented the true Israelites, who were also God's testimony. The final mention, in Revelation 1, pictures the church as the golden lampstand and as the testimony of God. (*Life Messages,* vol. 2, p. 244)

Today's Reading

The design of the lampstand is most meaningful. Though the lampstand is but one, there are six branches with seven lamps.... The lampstand signifies the Triune God. In typology gold represents the divine nature. Like gold, God's nature does not change or decay. That this lampstand was made of gold tells us that it represents God's nature. This gold was not in a formless lump. It was structured into a form that bespoke its function. The shape of the gold, a lampstand, symbolizes the image of God....Christ is called "the image of God" in 2 Corinthians 4:4. As the Son of God's love, He is "the image of the invisible God" (Col. 1:15). The image or form of the lampstand, then, signifies Christ.

What are the seven lamps? About this we cannot be clear until we come to Revelation. There we are plainly told that the seven lamps are the seven Spirits of God (Rev. 4:5). The seven Spirits are simply the Holy Spirit of God. These lamps are the expression or manifestation of God.

The Father, then, is signified by the gold, the element of which the lamp was made. The Son is signified by the form of the lampstand. The Spirit is the expression, as indicated by the seven lamps. Now do you agree that the golden lampstand pictures the Triune God?

By the time we come to Revelation, the church has become the lampstand. This means that the church is the expression of the Triune God. Each local church is a golden lampstand. What firstly signified the Triune God now depicts the church!

How can we, who are men of dust or clay, become a golden lampstand? When we were regenerated, we were born of God. Not only were our sins cleansed by the precious blood; there was also within us the element of the Father, just as a new baby has the life and nature of his father. Now there is gold, the element of God, in us!

Nonetheless, this gold needs to be formed. Paul travailed for the Galatians "until Christ is formed in you" (Gal. 4:19). It was not enough for Christ to be revealed in them (Gal. 1:16) or even to be living in them (Gal. 2:20). The gold had to take shape. (*Life Messages,* vol. 2, pp. 245-246)

As the seed of the truth concerning the lampstand in Exodus, the lampstand is Christ. The growth of this seed in Zechariah is that the lampstand is the Spirit. In Revelation is the harvest of the truth concerning the lampstand. The seed was one lampstand and the harvest is seven lampstands. The harvest is always a multiplication of the seed, so the seed has been multiplied from one into seven. The seed is Christ, the growth is the Spirit, and the harvest is the church. Hallelujah for Christ, the Spirit, and the church! The lampstand first signifies Christ, then the Spirit, and ultimately the church. This indicates that the very Christ is the Spirit and that the Spirit with the very Christ produces the churches. The lampstand in Exodus, the lampstand in Zechariah, and the lampstands in Revelation are three stages of the truth concerning the lampstand. (*The Church—the Reprint of the Spirit,* p. 9)

Further Reading: Life Messages, vol. 2, msg. 69

Enlightenment and inspiration: _____

_____

_____

_____

Morning Nourishment

Zech. ...There is a lampstand all of gold;...and *there are* two
4:2-3 olive trees beside it, one to the right of the bowl and
one to the left.

6 ...This is the word of Jehovah to Zerubbabel, saying,
Not by might nor by power, but by My Spirit, says
Jehovah of hosts.

The lampstand signifies Christ....But the lampstand also typifies something further. The "nursery" for all the seeds of the bib-
lical truths is not only the book of Genesis but also the first five
books of the Bible, the Pentateuch written by Moses....The first mention of the lampstand is not in Genesis but in Exodus (25:31-37).
Then the lampstand is mentioned in 1 Kings as an item in the
temple built by Solomon (7:49). Eventually, the lampstand is mentioned again in Zechariah related to the recovered temple (4:2).
Zechariah is a record of the recovery of the destroyed temple. The
lampstand in the tabernacle in Exodus signifies Christ Himself.
But the lampstand in Zechariah signifies the Spirit. Zechariah 4
tells us that when Zechariah saw the lampstand, he asked the
angel what this was. Then the angel answered, "This is the word
of Jehovah to Zerubbabel, saying, Not by might nor by power, but
by My Spirit, says Jehovah of hosts" (v. 6). The Lord told Zechariah that the lampstand was His Spirit. In Exodus the lampstand
was Christ. In Zechariah the lampstand was the Spirit. (*The
Church—the Reprint of the Spirit*, p. 9)

Today's Reading

For centuries, however, no one has seen, not even the deeper
saints, that the church is the reproduction of Christ. We can say
this because the lampstand in Exodus was one, and the lampstands in Revelation are seven. The one lampstand has been
reproduced. The unique lampstand in Exodus became a model,
out of which came seven lampstands. The seven lampstands are
exactly the same as the unique lampstand in nature, essence,
shape, and in every respect. Cakes may be made by putting the
batter into a mold. By using the mold the same cake may be made

again and again. Christ is the mold and the church is the reproduction of Christ....To say that the church is the Body, and the continuation, the enlargement, and the spreading of Christ is not enough. We all have to see that the church is an exact reproduction of Christ. Christ was the unique lampstand, and all the churches are the lampstands in the same nature, essence, model, shape, and function. According to the lampstand in Exodus we can say that the church is the reproduction of Christ, and according to the lampstand in Zechariah the church is the reprint of the Spirit. The ultimate definition of the church is that the church is the reproduction of Christ and the reprint of the Holy Spirit.

When we say that we are the church, we have to realize that the church is the reproduction of Christ and the reprint of the Spirit. When we say that we are the church, we must realize that we have to be fully in the Spirit. Even if we are only partially in the flesh, we become a poor reproduction, a poor reprint. When we brothers and sisters come together, if we all are in the Spirit, we are the church....Whether or not we are actually the church depends upon whether or not we are in the Spirit....Are we standing as the church in our locality? Then we must be in the Spirit. If we are not in the Spirit, we are through with the church because the church is the reproduction of Christ and the reprint of the Spirit.

Before [the Lord] wrote the seven epistles to the seven churches, He showed John a picture of seven golden lampstands (Rev. 1:11-12).... The church is nothing less than Christ and the Spirit because both Christ and the Spirit are the lampstand, and the church is also the lampstand. This is a picture of regeneration and transformation. Christ has been regenerated into our being, and we are being fully transformed into His Being (2 Cor. 3:18)....If we see this vision of the church, we will be afraid to exercise our flesh. We need to see that the church is absolutely something of Christ and in the Spirit. It is the lampstand, a reproduction of Christ and a reprint of the Spirit. (*The Church—the Reprint of the Spirit,* pp. 11-12)

Further Reading: The Church—the Reprint of the Spirit, ch. 1

Enlightenment and inspiration: _____

_____

_____

_____

Morning Nourishment

1 Cor. For also in one Spirit we were all baptized into one
12:13 Body, whether Jews or Greeks, whether slaves or
free, and were all given to drink one Spirit.

Gal. I am crucified with Christ; and *it is* no longer I *who*
2:20 live, but *it is* Christ *who* lives in me; and the *life*
which I now live in the flesh I live in faith, the *faith*
of the Son of God, who loved me and gave Himself
up for me.

We need to see [that] the Spirit is for the Body. The Spirit is
for many positive items of the Christian life, but ultimately the
Spirit is for the Body. The Spirit is for regeneration, sanctification, transformation, life, power, and so many spiritual items,
but all of these items are altogether for one issue—the Body.
Regeneration, sanctification, transformation, life, power, and
every positive spiritual blessing are for the Body. If we miss the
Body, we miss everything. If we miss the Body, we miss the mark
and the goal of God's economy.

The Spirit is for the Body, so 1 Corinthians 12:13 says that in
one Spirit we were all baptized into one Body, and Ephesians 4:4
says, "One Body and one Spirit." The one Spirit equals the one
Body, and the one Body equals the one Spirit. Thus, it is absolutely correct to say that the church is the reprint of the Spirit.
"No Spirit, no church. More Spirit, more church." This is because
the church is the reprint of the Spirit. The Spirit is the ultimate
consummation of the processed Triune God, and the church is the
reprint of the Spirit, the corporate expression of the processed Triune God. (*The Church—the Reprint of the Spirit,* pp. 20-21)

Today's Reading

If our eyes are opened by the Lord, and we see this vision concerning the church, this vision will be better than a thousand
messages concerning the church. If you have really seen this
vision, you will not exercise your mind to argue with the brothers
in your locality. When the sisters are exercising their emotions to

do something, this vision will terminate them. Even at the dining table this vision will be shining to govern us. We need a governing vision that terminates, kills, and annuls everything of our natural man. When a brother is about to exchange words with his wife, this vision will terminate him. When you are about to vindicate yourself, the Lord may say, "What's that?—natural!" If this vision is shining so brightly within us, the Lord will have a way to speak to us in our daily life to terminate our natural man. He will be able to say: "What's that?—natural love! What's that?—natural thinking! What's that?—your natural man! What's that?—natural, natural, natural!" Everything that is natural has to go. Otherwise, we actually are not in the church. Although you were put into the church nineteen and a half centuries ago, actually today you may not be in the church. Where are you? You may be in the natural life. We have to rise up to testify that the church is the reprint of the Spirit. We need to testify, "From now on, my natural being has no share in the church, no part in the church, because I have seen that the church is the reprint of the Spirit!" The church as the lampstand is pure and without mixture. The church is the embodiment of Christ and the reprint of the Spirit.

There is no comparison between the church and the denominations. The church is built with gold, pearls, and precious stones (Rev. 21:18-21). The church has nothing to do with the materials of wood, hay, and stubble produced by us in the natural man and the flesh (1 Cor. 3:12). We need to be warned in this matter. We should not insult the church by behaving and acting by our natural life. If we are in the church and still behave, act, and move by our natural being, by our natural life, this is an insult to the church life. The "good manners" for the church life is our reborn, indwelt spirit (John 3:6; Rom. 8:16; 2 Tim. 4:22). In our spirit, we have the reprint of the divine Spirit, which is the church in practicality. May the Lord open our eyes to see what the church is! (*The Church—the Reprint of the Spirit,* pp. 26-27)

Further Reading: The Church—the Reprint of the Spirit, chs. 2-3

Enlightenment and inspiration: _____

_____

_____

_____

Morning Nourishment

Zech. ...Upon one stone are seven eyes....And I will re-
3:9 move the iniquity of that land in one day.
4:10 ...For these seven rejoice when they see the plummet in the hand of Zerubbabel; they are the eyes of
Jehovah running to and fro on the whole earth.
Rev. And I saw...a Lamb standing as having *just* been
5:6 slain, having...seven eyes, which are the seven
Spirits of God sent forth into all the earth.

[In Zechariah 4:10] "these seven," which are the eyes of Jehovah, are the seven eyes on the stone in 3:9. The seven eyes of the stone are the seven eyes of Jehovah and also the seven eyes of the Lamb, Christ (Rev. 5:6). Thus, the stone, Jehovah, and the Lamb are one. Christ is the redeeming Lamb and the building stone, and He is also Jehovah. The seven eyes of Christ are the seven Spirits of God (see footnotes 5 on Rev. 5:6 and 5 on Rev. 1:4), indicating that Christ and the Holy Spirit, although distinct, are not separate. Just as a person's eyes are essentially one with the person, so the Holy Spirit is essentially one with Christ (Rom. 8:9-10; 2 Cor. 3:17). The function of Christ's seven eyes is to observe and search in order to execute God's judgment on the universe and to transfuse and infuse all that God is into His chosen people. In His resurrection Christ, as the last Adam, became the life-giving Spirit (1 Cor. 15:45b; John 6:63a; 2 Cor. 3:6b), who is also the sevenfold intensified Spirit. This Spirit is the Spirit of life (Rom. 8:2). Hence, the function of the seven Spirits is to impart the divine life into God's people for the building up of God's eternal habitation, the New Jerusalem. (Zech. 4:10, footnote 1)

Today's Reading

The seven lamps are the seven eyes of Christ as the Lamb and as the stone (Zech. 4:2, 10; Rev. 5:6; Zech. 3:9). Zechariah 3 tells us that Christ as the building stone has seven eyes, and Revelation 5 tells us that Christ as the redeeming Lamb has seven eyes. This proves that the Lamb is the stone and the stone is the Lamb. The Lamb is for redemption, and the stone is for building. For the purposes of redemption and building, Christ has seven eyes. (*The Church—the Reprint of the Spirit,* p. 28)

The church as the lampstand has seven lamps, which are God's seven Spirits. God is Spirit (John 4:24). More than this, we are told in Proverbs 20:27, "The spirit of man is the lamp of Jehovah." Within us, then, we have two lamps, the Spirit of God and our human spirit. Inside our little lamp is a stronger lamp. Before we were saved, our spirit was a broken lamp. After we repented, the lamp was restored and began to give forth light. Day by day as we prayed, the shining increased. With regeneration this lamp also had another lamp come into it. This was the Spirit of God. It is because of these two lamps that there is so much shining within us. The two become one, for "he who is joined to the Lord is one spirit" (1 Cor. 6:17).

Man's spirit, Proverbs 20:27 goes on to say, searches all his inward parts, or, as Darby's footnote says, "all the chambers of the soul."…The spirit is searching the chamber of your emotions, and of your mind, and of your will. Though we all have the pure gold in us, the inward parts of our soul may not be open. When we pray, we are afraid to open our emotion, for example, to the Lord. After we reach a certain point in our praying, we close up because we are unwilling to open some inner chamber to Him. We may faithfully attend all the meetings, read the Word, and spend time in prayer. Yet there is a door within that is locked. We are aware of this, yet we tell the Lord that there is no way to open that door, even though we love Him and have paid a price in other ways.

To have our spirit regenerated is simple. We confess our sins and receive the Lord. Then we have the Spirit of God within. To be transformed in our soul, however, is not easy. It needs the lamp of the Lord to search all the inner chambers. There are very few who have opened all their inner chambers to Him. (*Life Messages,* vol. 2, pp. 238-239)

Further Reading: Life-study of Revelation, msg. 33; *Life Messages,* vol. 2, msgs. 68, 70

Enlightenment and inspiration: _____

_____
_____
_____

Morning Nourishment

Rev. ...And *there were* seven lamps of fire burning before
4:5 the throne, which are the seven Spirits of God.
22:1 And he showed me a river of water of life, bright as
crystal, proceeding out of the throne of God and of
the Lamb in the middle of its street.

Christ and the Spirit are revealed in Revelation to carry out
God's economy. First, this carrying out of God's economy involves
administrating the entire situation in this universe and mainly administrating the world situation. All the international affairs are
neither in the hands of the diplomats nor in the hands of the
United Nations. The deciding place is on the throne....By my reading and studying of the world situation over the past sixty years, I
fully realize that the throne of God in the heavens is the deciding
factor of the world situation....All of the world leaders are under
the flaming of the seven Spirits. The seven Spirits are burning on
this earth today for the carrying out of God's administration. Christ
carries out His mission as the Ruler of the kings of the earth by the
seven burning Spirits....Today the seven Spirits of God are burning
not only concerning the churches but also concerning the world situation for the churches. The entire world situation is under the
flame of the burning of the seven Spirits. The seven Spirits today
are carrying out God's administration on this earth. The world situation, the international affairs, are all under the direction of this
flame. (*God's New Testament Economy,* pp. 240-241)

Today's Reading

The purpose of the burning flame in carrying out God's economy is to bring forth the golden lampstands, the churches. Burning
implies judging, purifying, refining, and producing. Never be disappointed by the rottenness, corruption, and immorality of today's
human society. Do not be disappointed or so concerned for the
world situation. Also, do not be disappointed by the weakness of the
local churches. I do not believe in the seemingly disappointing condition in the world or in the churches. I believe in the flame of the
burning seven Spirits which control and direct the world and

which also judge, purify, and refine the church to produce a pure golden lampstand. We are here endeavoring to afford the Lord a chance and an entrance to judge us, purify us, and refine us to produce a pure golden lampstand....We all need to pray, "Dear divine Flame, come! Come and judge! Come and purify! Come and refine that You may produce the golden lampstand." Nearly all the doors are closed to Christ in today's situation. By His mercy, though, we are open to Him. Every day, every morning, and every evening, we need to pray, "Lord, come; we are open to You! We open every avenue of our being to You."...Are you like this or do you shut yourself up and hide something from Him? We all need to pray, "Lord, we are open. Come and shine upon us and shine from within us and enlighten every avenue and every corner of our being. I like to be exposed, purged, and purified." Then the Lord has a way to produce a pure golden lampstand. The burning is going on not only in the entire world situation, but also in the churches. The more I read the newspapers, the more I get confirmed that the flaming Spirits direct the world situation, and also this flaming purifies the church to produce the golden lampstands.

The seven Spirits who are the lamps of fire in this age, executing God's New Testament economy (Rev. 4:5), will become the river of water, saturating the holy city of God, the New Jerusalem (22:1-2). First, the seven Spirits are the lamps of fire, and eventually the seven Spirits will be the river of water. Fire and water both refer to the same Spirit. Fire is to purge, refine, and produce, and water is to saturate and to supply. The Spirit is the refining fire in this age, and the Spirit is also the saturating, supplying water, first in this age and then in the coming age and eternity. The refining fire produces the lampstands, the churches, in this age with the saturating water, which will consummate in the New Jerusalem. Both the lampstand and the New Jerusalem are the full expression of God and the testimony of Jesus, in this age and in eternity. (*God's New Testament Economy,* pp. 241-242, 245)

Further Reading: God's New Testament Economy, ch. 23

Enlightenment and inspiration: _____

_____

_____

_____

Morning Nourishment

Zech. And *there are* two olive trees beside it, one to the
4:3 right of the bowl and one to the left.
12, 14 ...What are the two olive branches that are by the
side of the two golden spouts, which empty the gold
from themselves?...And he said, These are the two
sons of oil, who stand by the Lord of the whole earth.

[In] Zechariah 4:3...these two olive trees signify Joshua the
high priest and Zerubbabel the governor at the time, who were
the two sons of oil, filled with the Spirit of Jehovah for the rebuilding of God's temple (vv. 3-6, 12-14). The two sons of oil are also the
two witnesses in the last three and a half years of the present age,
who will be witnesses of God in the great tribulation for the
strengthening of God's peoples—the Israelites and the believers in
Christ (Rev. 11:3-12; 12:17). These two witnesses are...Moses, representing the law, and Elijah, representing the prophets; both
testify for God. The expression "the law and the prophets" (Luke
16:16) refers to the Old Testament....These two, Moses and Elijah,
will support and supply the persecuted Israelites and the believers
during the great tribulation. (*Life-study of Zechariah*, p. 28)

Today's Reading

[Zechariah 4:12 says that the] branches "empty the gold from
themselves." To empty the gold is to cause the gold to flow out. The
word *gold* here refers to the oil. The oil and the gold are one. The oil
denotes the Spirit, and the Spirit is God....In typology gold signifies God. The gold that fills the bowl is the Spirit; the Spirit is God; and
God is typified by gold. As we apply this matter to our experience
today, we see that the Spirit who flows out of us is God, and God is
gold. Thus, when we minister Christ to others, supplying them
with oil, we are actually supplying them with God. God is flowing
out from us into them. We all should be olive trees emptying God
from ourselves into others. In this way oil will be provided to the
needy by those who are olive trees out of which God is flowing.

The topstone with shouts of "Grace, grace to it" [v. 7] signifies

Christ, who is the grace as the stone, upon which are the seven eyes of Jehovah, the sevenfold intensified Spirit of God for the completion of the rebuilding of God's temple (3:9; 4:7-10; Rev. 5:6). To bring forth the topstone is to complete the building. This topstone is a type of Christ. For God's building Christ is a stone in three aspects. Christ is the foundation stone to uphold God's building (Isa. 28:16; 1 Cor. 3:11), the cornerstone to join together the Gentile and Jewish members of His Body (Eph. 2:20; 1 Pet. 2:6), and the topstone to consummate everything of God's building.

The shouts of "Grace, grace to it" indicate that the topstone itself is grace. The topstone is grace from God to us, and this grace is Christ.... [John 1:14] reveals that in His incarnation Christ brought God to us first as grace and then as reality. Grace is God in the Son as our enjoyment....When God is enjoyed by us, we have grace....The topstone is therefore the Christ who is the grace from God to us to be the covering of God's building. (*Life-study of Zechariah,* pp. 29-31)

In this lampstand there are only two basic elements—the gold and the oil. The gold is the solid form and the oil is the burning element. When these two are put together, there is a lampstand shining to express God in His Trinity with the Father's nature and essence, the Son's image and appearance, and the Spirit's expression. On the negative side, the priest snuffs all the negative things. On the positive side, the priest also functions to add more oil to the lampstand. Zechariah 4:12 tells us that the oil of the lampstand is golden oil. The two elements of the lampstand are the golden element and the element of the oil, but according to Zechariah these two elements actually are one. The oil itself is golden oil, which means that the gold flows as oil. When more oil is added into the lampstand, that means that more gold is added. The church as the lampstand is the solid embodiment of the Triune God with the sevenfold Spirit as the oil. Actually, the essence of the oil is the element of the gold. (*The Divine Economy,* p. 128)

Further Reading: Life-study of Zechariah, msg. 5; *The Divine Economy,* pp. 130-131*

Enlightenment and inspiration: _____

_____
_____
_____

Hymns, #1122

1   "Seven Spirits" of our God—
Lo, the age has now been turned
To the Spirit with the Son.
For the churches He's concerned.

      Come, O seven Spirits, come,
Thy recovery work be done!
Burn and search us thoroughly,
All the churches are for Thee.
    Burn us, search us,
All the churches are for Thee!

2   Sevenfold the Spirit is
For the deadness of the church,
That the saints may turn and live,
That the Lord may burn and search.

3   Now the Spirit of our God
Has become intensified:
'Tis not one but sevenfold
That the church may be supplied!

4   Now the seven Spirits are
Seven lamps of burning fire,
Not to teach us, but to burn,
Satisfying God's desire.

5   See the seven Spirits now—
Seven piercing, searching eyes.
In the church exposing us,
All the church He purifies.

6   Seven Spirits doth the Lord
For the churches now employ;
All those in the local church
May this Spirit now enjoy.

Composition for prophecy with main point and sub-points: _____

_____

_____

_____

_____

_____

_____

_____

_____

_____

_____

_____

_____

_____

_____

_____

_____

_____

_____

_____

_____

_____

_____

_____

_____

_____

_____

_____

_____

_____

_____

_____

_____

_____

_____

A Word concerning the Human Spirit and Aspects of Christ Unveiled in Zechariah for His Move on Earth

Scripture Reading: Zech. 2:1-2, 5, 8-9, 11; 10:1, 3; 11:7; 12:1, 10

Day 1 **I. "The burden of the word of Jehovah concerning Israel. Thus declares Jehovah, who stretches forth the heavens and lays the foundations of the earth and forms the spirit of man within him" (Zech. 12:1):**

A. In His creation God made three crucial, equally important items—the heavens, the earth, and the spirit of man.

B. The heavens are for the earth, the earth is for man, and man was created by God with a spirit that he may contact God, receive God, worship God, live God, fulfill God's purpose for God, and be one with God.

C. The central government and most prominent part of man's being should be his spirit; a man who is ruled and controlled by his spirit is a spiritual man (1 Cor. 2:14-15; 3:1; 14:32; John 3:6; Eph. 3:16; 1 Pet. 3:4; Dan. 6:3, 10).

D. In His economy God planned to have Christ as the centrality and universality of His move on earth; for His chosen people, who would care for Him as the Creator and as the Redeemer, there was the need for God to create a receiving organ so that they would have the capacity to receive all that He had planned for Christ to be.

E. Hence, Zechariah charges us to pay full attention to our human spirit so that we may receive the Christ revealed in this book and may understand all that is revealed therein concerning Him (Eph. 1:17-18a; 3:5; Gen. 2:7; Isa. 42:5; John 4:24; Phil. 4:23).

F. The way to fulfill God's economy in the divine history is by Christ as the sevenfold intensified

Spirit in our spirit; Zechariah reveals that the building of the church will be consummated by Christ as the sevenfold intensified Spirit of grace to be the topstone of grace (4:6-7, 12-14; 3:9; 12:1, 10; Rev. 4:5; 5:6).

Day 2 II. **We need to exercise our spirit to experience and enjoy Christ as the sevenfold intensified Spirit in the following aspects:**

A. Christ is a man with a measuring line in His hand, measuring God's people in order to test, judge, examine, and possess them for His kingdom (Zech. 2:1-2; Ezek. 40:3; 47:1-5; Psa. 139:23-24).

B. "I will be her wall of fire round about, declares Jehovah, and I will be the glory within her" (Zech. 2:5):

1. That the wall of the city of Jerusalem and the glory within her will be Jehovah Himself indicates that Jehovah as Christ will be the protection of Jerusalem at her circumference and her glory at her center; this shows the centrality and universality of Christ in God's economy.

2. Today Christ is the glory in the center of the church, and He is also the fire burning around the circumference of the church for her protection; in the New Jerusalem the Triune God in Christ will be the glory at its center (Rev. 21:23; 22:1, 5), and this glory will shine through the transparent wall of the city to be its protection of fire (21:11, 18a, 24).

C. Christ is the One sent by Jehovah of hosts and is also the Sender, Jehovah of hosts, for the care of His people, who are very dear to Him; whoever touches them touches the pupil of His eye (Zech. 2:8-9, 11; cf. John 14:26; 15:26).

Day 3 D. Christ came as a Shepherd, shepherding in Favor (grace) and Bonds (binding); grace is for our being mingled with God, and bonds are for our being bound into oneness (Zech. 11:7; 2:1-2, 5, 8-9, 11; John 21:15-17).

E. While the Lord is so favorable to us, we should ask Him to send us even more favor, more grace, more "rain" (Zech. 10:1; 12:10; Ezek. 34:26).

F. After being visited by the Lord as the Shepherd, every weak sheep among God's people becomes a horse of majesty (Zech. 10:3; cf. 9:13, 16; Dan. 11:32b).

G. Often during our time of morning revival, the Lord whistles to us, calling us and gathering us to Him; the Lord's whistling is not shrill but mild and gentle, somewhat like the singing of a bird (Zech. 10:8).

H. The Lord strengthens us in Himself so that we may walk about in His name (v. 12; Col. 3:17); "Jehovah will be King over all the earth; and in that day Jehovah will be the one God and His name the one name" (Zech. 14:9).

Day 4 III. **The focal point and major content of the divine history within human history are the two comings of Christ for the testimony of Jesus, the building of God:**

A. Zechariah 9 through 11 speaks of Christ's lowly first coming, which was humble and intimate:

1. Christ came as the King of Israel, lowly and riding upon a donkey, even upon a colt, the foal of a donkey (9:9-10; Matt. 21:5-10).

2. Christ came as a Shepherd, shepherding in Favor (grace) and Bonds (binding) (Zech. 11:7-11).

3. Christ was detested, attacked, rejected, and betrayed by one of His disciples for thirty pieces of silver (vv. 8, 12-13; Matt. 26:14-16; 27:3-10).

4. Christ was smitten as the Shepherd, and His disciples were scattered as the sheep (Zech. 13:7; Matt. 26:31).

5. Christ's two hands were wounded on the cross in the house of Israel, the house of those who love Him (Zech. 13:6; John 19:18a).

6. Christ's side was pierced, and He became an opened fountain for sin and for impurity (Zech. 12:10; 13:1; John 19:18a, 34; Matt. 26:28).

B. Zechariah 12 through 14 speaks of Christ's victorious second coming, which will be with power and authority:

1. Christ will come a second time accompanied by His saints, the overcomers (14:5; Joel 3:11; Jude 14).

2. His feet will stand on the Mount of Olives, which is before Jerusalem on the east (Zech. 14:4; Acts 1:9-12).

3. He will fight for the children of Israel, His chosen people, against the nations that besiege them and will save them from destruction (Zech. 14:2-3, 12-15; 12:1-9).

4. At that time the whole house of Israel will look upon Him whom they have pierced, and they will mourn for Him; thus, all Israel will be saved (vv. 10-14; Rom. 11:26).

5. Afterward, He will be the King to reign and rule over the nations; all the people will go up to Jerusalem year after year to worship Him, and all will be sanctified unto Him (Zech. 9:10; 14:16-21).

Day 5 IV. **The all-inclusive Christ is the history of God working within the history of man to gain the building of God for the manifestation of God (4:9; 6:12-15; Matt. 16:18; John 1:1, 14; 1 Cor. 15:45b; Rev. 4:5; 5:6; 21:2):**

A. While Christ is skillfully working to sovereignly control the world situation in human history, He is skillfully working Himself into us in the divine history to make us the masterpiece of His work, the poem of God, a new invention of God, expressing His infinite wisdom and divine design (Acts 5:31; Eph. 2:10).

B. Christ in His humanity is the Angel of Jehovah, Jehovah Himself as the Triune God, standing with God's people in the lowest part of the valley in their humiliation to care for them, intercede for them, and bring them swiftly out of Babylonian captivity (Zech. 1:7-17; Exo. 3:2, 4-6, 13-15; Isa. 63:9; Deut. 33:27).

C. Christ is the last Craftsman used by God to break the four horns; the four horns are the four kingdoms with their kings—Babylon, Medo-Persia, Greece, and the Roman Empire—also signified by the great human image with four sections in Daniel 2:31-33, the four stages of locusts in Joel 1:4, and the four beasts in Daniel 7:3-8, that damaged and destroyed the chosen people of God (Zech. 1:18-21):

1. The four craftsmen are the skills used by God to destroy these kingdoms with their kings; each of the first three kingdoms (Babylon, Medo-Persia, and Greece) was taken over in a skillful way by the kingdom that followed it (Dan. 5; 8:3-7).

2. The fourth Craftsman will be Christ as the stone cut out without hands, who will crush the restored Roman Empire and thereby crush the great human image as the totality of human government at His coming back (2:31-35).

3. This stone signifies not only the individual Christ but also the corporate Christ, Christ with His "mighty ones" (Joel 3:11).

D. In order to live in the divine history within the human history and become Christ's mighty ones for His building, we need to apply the cleansing blood of Christ, live in the divine Spirit of Christ, and abide in the beautifying and killing word of Christ to flow out Christ for the unique expression of Christ (Zech. 3:3-4; 1 John 1:9; Zech. 4:6; 12:1; Rev. 19:13-15; Eph. 5:26; 6:17; 1 Cor. 10:16; Zech. 4:12-14; John 7:37-39a).

Day 6   **V. The world situation has always been the**

indicator of the Lord's move on earth (cf. 1 Chron. 12:32a):

A. The mystery of lawlessness is working today among the nations and in human society; this lawlessness will culminate in the man of lawlessness, Antichrist (2 Thes. 2:3-12):

1. Antichrist will be the power of Satan, the embodiment of Satan; he will persecute and destroy the people of God—both the God-fearing Jews and the Christ-believing Christians (Dan. 8:24; Rev. 12:17; 13:7).

2. Antichrist will demolish and desolate the temple of God and the city of God; he will cast truth down to the ground (Dan. 9:27; 8:12).

3. Antichrist will have sharp insight to perceive things and will speak things against the Most High (7:8, 20, 25).

4. Antichrist will wear out the saints of the Most High (v. 25; cf. Mark 6:45-52).

5. Satan and Antichrist want the souls of men to be the instruments for their activities in the last age (Rev. 18:11-13; 2 Tim. 3:1-5; cf. Zech. 12:1).

B. The ten kings typified by the ten toes of the great image in Daniel 2 will be under Antichrist, who will be the last Caesar of the revived Roman Empire; all this will transpire in Europe (Rev. 17:10-14):

1. Before the crushing of Antichrist and the totality of human government transpires, the Lord's recovery must spread to Europe and be rooted there.

2. The spreading of the truths of the Lord's recovery will be a preparation for the Lord's coming back to bring the recovery and restoration not only to Israel but also to the entire creation (Matt. 24:14; cf. Rev. 5:6).

3. We should tell the Lord, "Lord, these days are the consummation of the age. Lord, in these days rekindle my love toward You."

Morning Nourishment

Zech. The burden of the word of Jehovah concerning
12:1   Israel. *Thus* declares Jehovah, who stretches forth
       the heavens and lays the foundations of the earth
       and forms the spirit of man within him.
John   God is Spirit, and those who worship Him must
4:24   worship in spirit and truthfulness.
1 Cor. But the spiritual man discerns all things, but he
2:15   himself is discerned by no one.

In His creation God made three crucial, equally important
items—the heavens, the earth, and the spirit of man. The heavens are for the earth, the earth is for man, and man was created
by God with a spirit that he may contact God, receive God, worship God, live God, fulfill God's purpose for God, and be one
with God. In His economy God planned to have Christ as the
centrality and universality of His move on earth. For His
chosen people, who would care for Him as the Creator and as
the Redeemer, there was the need for Him to create a receiving
organ so that they would have the capacity to receive all that
God had planned for Christ to be. Hence, [the book of Zecha-
riah] charges us to pay full attention to our human spirit, that
we may receive the Christ revealed in this book and may understand all that is revealed therein concerning Him (Eph. 1:17-
18a; 3:5). (Zech. 12:1, footnote 2)

Today's Reading

[In 1 Corinthians 2:14 the word *spiritually*] refers to the
spirit of man that is moved by the Spirit of God to fully exercise its function and thereby replace the human soul's rule
and control over man. It is only by such a spirit that man can
discern the things of the Spirit of God. A man who is ruled and
controlled by his spirit is a spiritual man, as mentioned in
[verse 15]. Since God is Spirit, all the things of the Spirit of
God are spiritual. Therefore, to discern, to know, the things
of the Spirit of God, man must use the human spirit (John
4:24). (1 Cor. 2:14, footnote 6)

Zechariah 12:1 says, "The burden of the word of Jehovah concerning Israel. Thus declares Jehovah, who stretches forth the heavens and lays the foundations of the earth and forms the spirit of man within him."...It is marvelous that such a verse as this is in an Old Testament book which unveils a Christ who is so involved with human history and politics. This indicates that in His economy God planned to have Christ as the centrality and universality of His move on earth. As the very God, He has ruled over the entire human race, managing the world situation age after age for thousands of years....Christ is wonderful, but if we did not have a spirit, how could we receive Him? Today in every circle of society, people do not exercise their spirit. Even in religious circles, the matter of the human spirit is neglected or even opposed and denied. If we neglect our human spirit, there is no way for us to contact God.

Zechariah is a book unveiling Christ as God's center and circumference, yet this Christ is intimately involved with human history. Not just anyone can know this One, but God's chosen people who realize that they have a spirit can know Him. In reading the book of Zechariah and in contacting the Christ revealed in this book, we must first know that we have a spirit. Then we need to exercise our spirit to pray, saying, "Lord, I want to gain the Christ who is unveiled in Zechariah." If we exercise our spirit in this way, we will sense something living touching us deep within. This is why there is in this book such a verse as 12:1, a verse that charges us to pay full attention to the receiver within us, our human spirit, that we may receive the Christ revealed in the book of Zechariah.

Though Zechariah was a young man, he knew the secret of contacting God to receive what God has revealed. We all need to learn of him to exercise our spirit to receive God and to receive what He has revealed. (*Life-study of Zechariah,* pp. 67-69)

Further Reading: Life-study of Zechariah, msg. 12

Enlightenment and inspiration: _____

_____

_____

_____

Morning Nourishment

Zech.   Then I lifted up my eyes and I looked, and there
2:1-2   was a man, and in His hand was a measuring line.
And I said, Where are you going? And He said to
me, To measure Jerusalem; to see how great its
breadth is and how great its length is.
  5 For I will be her wall of fire round about, declares
Jehovah, and I will be the glory within her.

That the wall of the city of Jerusalem and the glory within her
will be Jehovah Himself indicates that Jehovah as Christ will be
the protection of Jerusalem at her circumference and her glory at
her center. This shows the centrality and universality of Christ
in God's economy. Today Christ is the glory in the center of the
church, and He is also the fire burning around the circumference
of the church for her protection. In the New Jerusalem the Triune
God in Christ will be the glory at its center (Rev. 21:23; 22:1, 5), and
this glory will shine through the transparent wall of the city (Rev.
21:11, 18a, 24) to be its protection of fire. (Zech. 2:5, footnote 1)

Today's Reading

The Lamb [in Revelation 5:6], who is the stone in Zechariah
3:9, is Christ, and the seven eyes are the sevenfold intensified
Spirit. Thus, the Christ who has been engraved by God to take
away our sin bears the sevenfold intensified Spirit. Actually, He,
the last Adam, has become a life-giving Spirit (1 Cor. 15:45b),
even the sevenfold intensified Spirit. Christ today is the Spirit,
and we have a spirit particularly formed by God to match Christ.

In the first part of Zechariah (chs. 1—6), there are five visions
concerning Christ, and in the last part (chs. 9—14), many details concerning Christ....In the first of the five visions concerning Christ,
Christ is unveiled as the man as the Angel of Jehovah riding on a
red horse and standing among the myrtle trees (1:7-17). The myrtle trees signify the humiliated yet precious people of Israel in
their captivity. Christ's riding on a red horse indicates that He
was the redeeming One. His being the Angel of Jehovah indicates
that He was the One sent by God to take care of His people with

much expectation while they were in captivity.

In the second vision (vv. 20-21) Christ is the last Craftsman used by God to break the four horns—Babylon, Persia, Greece, and the Roman Empire—which damaged and destroyed the chosen people of God (vv. 18-19). Christ will be the unique One not only to break the four horns but also to smash the entire human government from the toes to the head, as signified by the great human image in Daniel 2.

In the next vision Christ is the One who measures Jerusalem in order to possess it (Zech. 2:1-2). This One not only possesses Jerusalem but also becomes the center of Jerusalem as the glory within her and the circumference of Jerusalem as the wall of fire round about her (v. 5). Furthermore, He is both the sending One and the sent One. He, Jehovah of hosts, has sent Himself as the Angel of Jehovah (vv. 8-9, 11).

In the fourth vision Christ is unveiled as the topstone of grace (4:7)....The fifth vision involving Christ is the vision of the lampstand of gold and the two olive trees (4:2-3, 11-14). The lampstand here signifies the nation of Israel as the collective testimony of God shining out all His virtues. We may say that this lampstand is also a type of Christ, the embodiment of the Triune God. In Zechariah's time the two olive trees were Joshua and Zerubbabel, but during the three and a half years of the great tribulation, the two olive trees will be Moses and Elijah.

The book of Zechariah reveals many things concerning Christ. First, the redeeming Christ, as a man and as the Angel of Jehovah, the embodiment of the Triune God, was sent by God to be with His humiliated people of Israel in their captivity, signified by the myrtle trees in the bottoms (1:8-11). Then Christ, as a man in His humanity, was the One sent by Jehovah of hosts and was also the Sender, Jehovah of hosts, dealing with the nations who plundered the people of Zion and touched them as touching the pupil of His eye (2:1, 8-10). (*Life-study of Zechariah,* pp. 93-95, 86)

Further Reading: Life-study of Zechariah, msgs. 14-15

Enlightenment and inspiration: _____

_____
_____
_____

Morning Nourishment

Zech. **So I shepherded the flock of slaughter, and there-**
11:7 **by the afflicted of the flock. And I took to myself**
two staffs; one I called Favor, and the other I called
Bonds; and I shepherded the flock.
10:8 **I will whistle for them and gather them, for I have**
redeemed them; and they will multiply as they have
multiplied.

[In Zechariah 11:7] *I* refers to Jehovah, as indicated by the previous verse. Jehovah as Jesus came to feed His people, who were about to be slaughtered, the afflicted of the flock.

Jehovah as Jesus brought two staffs—Favor and Bonds. Favor refers to grace, and Bonds refers to being bound into one-ness. Jesus came as the Shepherd to feed God's flock with grace so that they might have oneness. (Zech. 11:7, footnotes 1 and 2)

Today's Reading

"Ask rain of Jehovah / At the time of spring rain, / Of Jehovah who makes the lightning, / And He will give them showers of rain, / To everyone herbage in the field" (Zech. 10:1). The word *rain* here signifies blessing. To ask for more rain is to seek more blessing.... The Lord is encouraging the children of Israel to seek more blessings while He would be favorable to them. While the Lord is so favorable to us, we should ask Him to send us even more favor. Since God is giving us showers of rain, we should ask Him for more rain. This indicates that we all need to pray for the Lord's abundant blessing.

"Jehovah of hosts has visited His flock, the house of Judah, / And will make them like His horse of majesty in battle" (Zech. 10:3b). God came to His people in such a gracious way to visit them. His visiting them was Christ's coming to them. He came in the man, Jesus. Of course, chapter 10 does not mention the name Jesus Christ or Messiah, but the word *visited* here should be understood as Christ's coming. Two thousand years ago He came in the form of a man. This portion of the Word speaks about the Shepherd of God's flock. In the New Testament the Lord Jesus likened Himself to a shepherd. He came as the real Shepherd and blamed the other shepherds, who were the elders, the scribes, and the priests. They were the wrong shepherds, but the Lord Jesus was the unique Shepherd. He even told us that He was the good Shepherd who gave up His life for the sheep (John 10:11, 14-15). On the one hand, the Lord punished the false shepherds; on the other hand, He, the real Shepherd, has visited His flock. By visiting His flock He makes them like a horse of majesty....We all need to progress so that we are no longer sheep but horses of majesty. After being touched by the Shepherd, every weak sheep will become a horse of majesty.

Zechariah 10:8-12 reveals further aspects of the Lord's loving visitation to Israel....The Lord's whistling [in verse 8] is not shrill but mild and gentle, somewhat like the singing of a bird. Often during our time of morning revival, the Lord whistles to us, calling us and gathering us to Him.

Verse 12 concludes, "I will strengthen them in Jehovah, / And they will walk about in His name, / Declares Jehovah." The *I* here is Jehovah, indicating that Jehovah will strengthen His people in Himself. They will then walk about in His name. To be in someone's name is to be one with the person who is the reality of that name. To be in God's name is to be one with God in our daily walk, living, walking, and having our being in God's name.

All of chapter 10 talks about God's loving visitation. We need to realize and remember that this visitation is actually Christ's coming. I can testify from my experience that when we enjoy the Lord's loving visitation, our situation is exactly like that of God's people described in this chapter. Often after we enjoy such a loving visitation, our situation changes. In His visitation He encourages us to seek more blessings. We are little lambs, but after His loving visitation, we become horses. We are not that bold or strong, but after the Lord's visitation with His dear touch, we are strengthened to become horses of majesty in battle. Eventually, the Lord strengthens us in Himself so that we may walk about in His name. (*Life-study of Zechariah,* pp. 57-60)

Further Reading: Life-study of Zechariah, msg. 10

Enlightenment and inspiration: _____

_____

_____

_____

Morning Nourishment

Zech. **Exult greatly, O daughter of Zion; shout, O daugh-**
9:9-10 **ter of Jerusalem! Now your King comes to you. He**
        is righteous and bears salvation, lowly and riding
        upon a donkey, even upon a colt, the foal of a don-
        key;...and He will speak peace unto the nations,
        and His dominion will be from sea to sea and from
        the River unto the ends of the earth.

Zechariah 12—14...unveils Christ as the Messiah returning to be enthroned as the King not only over Israel but also over the whole world. His first coming, described in chapters 9—11, was humble and intimate; His [victorious] coming back, described in chapters 12—14, will be with power and authority. (Zech. 12:1, footnote 1)

In His first coming, Christ came as a lowly King and was temporarily welcomed as the King into Jerusalem in a lowly form. [Zechariah 9:9 speaks] regarding this....Christ came also as a Shepherd (11:7-11), shepherding in Favor (grace) and Bonds (binding). However, He, the proper Shepherd of Israel, was detested, attacked, rejected, and sold for thirty pieces of silver (vv. 12-13). (*Life-study of Zechariah*, p. 95)

Today's Reading

[Zechariah 13:6] speaks about the cross in a mysterious way. "Someone will say to Him, What are these wounds between Your arms? And He will say, Those with which I was wounded in the house of those who love Me."...The Lord came to the house of those who loved Him, yet they wounded Him, and the wounds are visible in His hands (KJV). This means that His hands were nailed to the cross. The Recovery Version says that He was wounded between His arms. This was the piercing of His side....You may say this was the wound on His hands, or you may also say that this was the wound between His two arms. Verse 1 gives us the purpose for which He was wounded: "In that day there will be an opened fountain...for sin and for impurity." This fountain is the flow of His precious blood from His hands and His side, the fountain for sin. Zechariah 12:10 says, "And I will pour out on the house of David and on the inhabitants of Jerusalem the Spirit of grace and of supplications; and they will look upon Me, whom they have pierced."

Zechariah also speaks of the Lord's second coming. "Indeed a day is coming for Jehovah when the spoil taken from you will be divided among you....Then Jehovah will go forth and fight against those nations, as when He fights in a day of battle. And His feet will stand in that day on the Mount of Olives, which is before Jerusalem on the east; and the Mount of Olives will be split at its middle toward the east and toward the west into a very great valley, so that half of the mountain will remove to the north and half of it to the south. And you will flee....And Jehovah my God will come, and all the saints with Him" (14:1, 3-5).

These verses tell us that He will come with all the saints to fight, and He will stand upon the Mount of Olives. If we read Acts 1:9-12, we see that the Lord Jesus ascended from the Mount of Olives, and the angels told the disciples that He will come back in the same way. He left from the Mount of Olives, and He will come back to the Mount of Olives. He will return to the very spot from which He ascended. At that time, the Jewish people will be surrounded by their enemies, just as they were at the side of the Red Sea. As the Lord split the Red Sea, in the future He will split the Mount of Olives into two parts, making an opening for the people to flee from their enemies.

While the Lord Christ will be fighting for the people of Israel, God will pour upon them the Spirit of grace, and all of them will repent and mourn. They will not mourn for their sins, but for their rejection of the Lord in the past. All the Hebrews will then repent and receive Him as Savior. He will solve all the problems on earth and be the King over all the nations. "Jehovah will be King over all the earth; and in that day Jehovah will be the one God and His name the one name" (Zech. 14:9). (*The Recovery of God's House and God's City,* pp. 59-61)

Further Reading: Life-study of Zechariah, msgs. 9, 11, 13; *The Recovery of God's House and God's City,* ch. 6

Enlightenment and inspiration: _____

_____

_____

_____

Morning Nourishment

Zech.   **Then I lifted up my eyes and looked, and there were**
1:18   **four horns.**
20-21   **Then Jehovah showed me four craftsmen. And I said, What do these come to do? And he spoke, saying, These are the horns that have so scattered Judah that no man lifts up his head, but these have come to terrify them, to cast down the horns of the nations who have lifted up the horn against the land of Judah to scatter it.**

The Greek word, *poiema,* means something that has been made, a handiwork, or something that has been written or composed as a poem. Not only a poetic writing may be considered a poem, but also any work of art that expresses the maker's wisdom and design. We, the church, the masterpiece of God's work, are a poem expressing God's infinite wisdom and divine design.

The heavens, the earth, and man, created by God, are not God's masterpiece; but the church, the Body of Christ, the fullness of the One who fills all in all (Eph. 1:23), the corporate and universal new man (v. 15), is a masterpiece. (Eph. 2:10, footnote 1)

We, the church, the masterpiece of God's work, are an absolutely new item in the universe, a new invention of God. We were created by God in Christ through regeneration to be His new creation (2 Cor. 5:17). (Eph. 2:10, footnote 2)

Christ, the redeeming One, was Israel's patron, ready to do anything for them swiftly in order to care for them in their captivity. Christ maintained Israel in their captivity that He might eventually be born into humanity through Israel to accomplish God's eternal economy. (Zech. 1:8, footnote 3)

Today's Reading

The vision of the four horns and the four craftsmen (Zech. 1:18-21) was a comforting and encouraging word of promise to Israel as God's answer to Christ's intercession for Zion and Jerusalem in verse 12. The four horns are the four kingdoms with their kings—Babylon, Medo-Persia, Greece, and the Roman Empire—

also signified by the great human image in Daniel 2:31-33 and by the four beasts in Daniel 7:3-8, that damaged and destroyed the chosen people of God. The four craftsmen (Zech. 1:20) are the skills used by God to destroy these four kingdoms with their kings. Each of the first three kingdoms—Babylon, Medo-Persia, and Greece—was taken over in a skillful way by the kingdom that followed it (cf. Dan. 5; 8:3-7). The fourth Craftsman will be Christ as the stone cut out without hands, who will crush the restored Roman Empire and thereby crush the great human image as the totality of human government at His coming back (Dan. 2:31-35). (Zech. 1:18, footnote 1)

As revealed in Joel 2:30-31a, God's saving of the returned Jews by pouring out His Spirit upon them the second time (see footnote 28[1], par. 1) will be accompanied by the natural calamities of the sixth seal and the first four trumpets (Rev. 6:12-17; 8:7-12) on the heavens, the sun, the moon, the stars, and the earth as a prelude to the great tribulation (Matt. 24:21). It will take place before the fifth trumpet, the first of the three woes (Rev. 8:13 and footnote), which are the major structure of the great tribulation, in the great and terrible day of Jehovah (Joel 2:31b). See footnote 1 on Revelation 6:12.

In spite of such an outpouring of the Spirit, many of the returned Jews will not believe but will continue to be stubborn. Eventually, during the tribulation, Jerusalem will be surrounded by the Gentile armies under Antichrist, whose intention will be to destroy Israel entirely (Zech. 14:2; Rev. 16:13-16). At that juncture the Lord Jesus Christ will descend with His overcomers, His mighty ones (Joel 3:11). Furthermore, according to Zechariah 12:10, at that time the consummated Spirit will again be poured out, and the remnant of the children of Israel will be saved. Thus, the three outpourings of the Holy Spirit—on the day of Pentecost, just before the great tribulation, and at the Lord's second coming—work together for the salvation of Israel. (Joel 2:30, footnote 1)

Further Reading: Life-study of Zechariah, msg. 15

Enlightenment and inspiration: _____

_____

_____

_____

Morning Nourishment

2 Thes. For *it is* the mystery of lawlessness *that* is now
2:7-8 operating, *but* only until the one now restraining
goes out of the way. And then the lawless one will
be revealed (whom the Lord Jesus will slay by
the breath of His mouth and bring to nothing by the
manifestation of His coming).

The lawlessness that will characterize Antichrist (2 Thes. 2: 3) is already operating in this age mysteriously. It is the mystery of lawlessness working today among the nations and in human society. (2 Thes. 2:7, footnote 1)

[In Daniel 7:7-8 the] beast had ten horns. A small horn came up among the ten horns, and three of them were uprooted from before it (vv. 8, 24). This signifies that a king will come up among the ten kings, and he will subdue three of the kings. This is a prophecy concerning the rising up of Antichrist....Daniel said that this horn had eyes like the eyes of a man and a mouth speaking great things (vv. 8, 20, 25). This signifies that Antichrist will have sharp insight to perceive things and a mouth to speak great things against God (Rev. 13:5-6). Daniel prophesied that Antichrist will be slain and that his body will be destroyed and given to the burning fire (Dan. 7:11; Rev. 19:20). Antichrist will wage war with the saints. He will wear out the saints of the Most High for three and a half years and prevail against them (Dan. 7:21, 25; Rev. 13:7). His intention will even be to change the times and the law (Dan. 7:25). But he will be judged by God, and his dominion will be taken away, "so as to annihilate and destroy it unto the end" (v. 26). According to 7:22 and 27 the kingdom and the dominion and the greatness of the kingdoms under heaven will eventually be given to the saints of the Most High. (*Truth Lessons—Level Four*, vol. 2, p. 121)

Today's Reading

It is a historical fact that the world situation has always been the indicator of the Lord's move on earth....It is correct to say that the history in the Bible is centered around Israel, but the Bible is not just a history of the Jews. The Bible is a history of

God's economy. Israel has been the center of the carrying out of God's economy on earth. God is not interested merely in the history of the Jews. His interest is in His economy which is being carried out by Him on earth. The carrying out of His economy has much to do with the world situation.

Europe, in the consummation of the fulfillment of the vision concerning the great human image in Daniel 2, is also more vitally crucial than any other country and race—the crushing of the two feet of the great human image will be the crushing of the entire human government (vv. 34-35)....The periods of history signified by the head, the breast and the arms, the belly and the thighs, and the legs have been fulfilled. But the ten toes have not been fulfilled. According to Revelation 17:12, ten kings will be raised up before the great tribulation in the revived Roman Empire. They will be one with Antichrist in opposing God and persecuting His people—the Jews and the believers. These ten kings are likened to the ten toes of the great image seen by Nebuchadnezzar in his dream (Dan. 2:42). They will submit themselves and their kingdom to Antichrist (Rev. 17:17).

We need to see [the crushing of the image and its ten toes] as a basis to understand the Lord's mind. Before this crushing transpires, the Lord's recovery must spread to Europe and be rooted there. The spreading of the truths of the Lord's recovery will be a preparation for the Lord's coming back to bring the recovery and restoration not only to Israel but also to the entire creation.

Europe still remains as a region in which the Lord's recovery needs to be rooted and grow. I hope that we would bring this fellowship to the Lord and pray. We should tell the Lord, "Lord, these days are the consummation of the age. Lord, in these days rekindle my love toward You." (*The World Situation and the Direction of the Lord's Move*, pp. 8, 18-19)

Further Reading: The Collected Works of Watchman Nee, vol. 10, pp. 423-433, 466-478, 481-485; *The World Situation and the Direction of the Lord's Move*, ch. 1; *Life-study of Revelation*, msgs. 40, 42

Enlightenment and inspiration: _____

_____

_____

_____

Hymns, #782

1   How mysterious, O Lord,
    That Thy Spirit dwells in mine;
    O how marvelous it is,
    Into one, two spirits twine.

2   By the spirit I can walk,
    Spiritual in spirit be;
    By the spirit I can serve,
    And in spirit worship Thee.

3   Thru Thy Word and by my prayer
    In the spirit touching Thee,
    Lifted high my spirit is,
    Strengthened shall my spirit be.

4   Make my spirit strong I pray
    Others' spirits to revive;
    Lift my spirit high and free,
    Others' spirits then may thrive.

5   Every time I speak, O Lord,
    May my spirit actuate;
    And whatever I may do,
    Let my spirit motivate.

6   Every time my spirit acts
    Others' spirits opened be,
    Every time my spirit moves
    Others' lifted unto Thee.

7   Lord, have mercy, from above
    May Thy Spirit breathe on me;
    Then my spirit will be rich,
    Strengthened and refreshed by Thee.

Composition for prophecy with main point and sub-points: _____

_____

_____

_____

_____

_____

_____

_____

_____

_____

_____

_____

_____

_____

_____

_____

_____

_____

_____

_____

_____

_____

_____

_____

_____

_____

_____

_____

_____

_____

_____

_____

_____

_____

_____

_____

The Evil and Wickedness of Commerce versus a Divine Sense of Value concerning Christ and the Church

Scripture Reading: Zech. 5:5-11; Luke 16:13; Phil. 3:7-8; Acts 20:28

Day 1

I. **The vision of the ephah vessel signifies the evil and wickedness of business, or commerce, on the earth (Zech. 5:5-11):**
   A. Commerce seems to have a proper appearance; actually, commerce is evil, full of wickedness (vv. 6-8):
      1. The vision of the ephah vessel shows us that the most evil thing on earth is commerce (vv. 5-11).
      2. The woman sitting within the ephah vessel signifies the wickedness contained in commerce, such as covetousness, deceit, and the love of money (vv. 7-8a).
      3. This vision corresponds to that of Babylon the Great in Revelation 18; these two visions show that in the sight of God the wickedness contained in commerce is a form of idolatry and fornication:
         a. The beginning of commerce is connected with Satan, and its end, with Babylon (Ezek. 28; Rev. 18):
            (1) Ezekiel 28 is the beginning of world commerce, and Revelation 18 is the consummation, the peak development, of world commerce.
            (2) The most severe judgment from God will be brought against Babylon because it will be the consummation of aggrandizement by trade and the epitome of sin (vv. 2-3, 5, 15-17a, 20).
         b. Commerce is the field in which, more than any other, "the corruption which is in the

world by lust" (2 Pet. 1:4) relentlessly pur-
sues even the most high-principled of
Christians and can easily overtake them to
their undoing (Neh. 5:1-13; 13:10-14).

Day 2   4. Building a house for the woman in the land
of Shinar signifies that God's sovereignty
will cause the wickedness in business, which
the people of Israel learned from the Babylonians in their captivity, to go back to Babylon (Zech. 5:9-11).

B. We need to be delivered from the commercial
mind (Matt. 19:27—20:16):

1. Satan is a businessman, a merchant, and his
thought is according to his commercial principle (Job 1:9-11; Ezek. 28:16, 18; cf. Rev. 18:2-5,
9-19).

2. Peter's concept in dealing with the Lord in
Matthew 19:27 was commercial, according
to the principle of work; in His answer to
Peter the Lord strongly indicated that His
reward is not commercial but according to
His desire and grace (v. 28—20:16):

a. Peter's natural concept, representing that
of all believers, was commercial (vv. 11-12).

b. The Lord's word in verse 14 shattered
Peter's natural, commercial mind and
destroyed his concept of commerce
(16:23-26; 2 Cor. 10:4-5).

Day 3   C. "No household servant can serve two masters;
for either he will hate the one and love the other,
or he will hold to one and despise the other. You
cannot serve God and mammon" (Luke 16:13):

1. Mammon stands in opposition to God, indicating that wealth, or riches, is the opponent of God, robbing God's people of their
service to Him.

2. To serve the Lord requires us to love Him,
giving our heart to Him, and requires us to
cleave to Him, giving our entire being to

Him (Matt. 6:19-21):

    a. In this way we are released from being occupied and usurped by mammon so that we may serve the Lord wholly and fully (4:10).

    b. In order to serve the Lord, we must overcome the enticing, deceitful mammon of unrighteousness (Luke 16:9, 13; Matt. 13:22).

  3. Giving money and material things in resurrection is a strong indication that we are under God's administration in resurrection and have overcome the possession of material riches (1 Cor. 16:1-3; Acts 2:44-45; 4:32-35; 11:29).

D. "Let your way of life be without the love of money" (Heb. 13:5a):

  1. Whatever one loves, his whole heart, even his entire being, is set on and occupied and fully possessed by (cf. Mark 12:30; 2 Tim. 3:1-2a).

  2. "Those who intend to be rich fall into temptation and a snare and many foolish and harmful desires, which plunge men into destruction and ruin" (1 Tim. 6:9).

  3. Because of the love of money, some have been led away from the faith and have pierced themselves through with many pains (v. 10).

Day 4 **II. We need to have a divine sense of value in order to appreciate the supreme preciousness of Christ and the exceeding worth of the church (Luke 16:15b; 1 Pet. 2:4, 7; Matt. 13:45-46; Acts 20:28):**

A. The Bible has much to say concerning a change in one's concept of value (Psa. 118:22; 1 Cor. 1:18; Matt. 6:32-33; 10:37-38; 16:26; 18:8-9; 20:25-27; Job 22:23-28; Heb. 11:24-26):

  1. Before a person believes in the Lord, his concept of value is perverted, but once a person

is saved, his concept of value changes (Luke 19:2, 8-9).

2. If we have a thorough change in our concept of value, we will know to choose the most excellent portion (10:41-42; Matt. 26:6-13).

B. We need to appreciate the supreme preciousness of Christ (Mark 14:3-9):

1. "Coming to Him, a living stone,...with God chosen and precious"; "to you therefore who believe is the preciousness" (1 Pet. 2:4, 7a):

a. In verse 4 *precious* indicates preciousness that is recognized and held in honor.

b. The Christ chosen by God as a stone, even a cornerstone that is precious to God, is the preciousness to the believers (v. 7a).

c. We need to have a vision of the preciousness of Christ (vv. 4, 7a).

Day 5

2. "What things were gains to me, these I have counted as loss on account of Christ. But moreover I also count all things to be loss on account of the excellency of the knowledge of Christ Jesus my Lord, on account of whom I have suffered the loss of all things and count them as refuse that I may gain Christ" (Phil. 3:7-8):

a. We need to know Christ in His excellency, in His supreme preciousness; no person, matter, or thing is more precious than the Lord Jesus as the treasure within us (2 Cor. 4:7; S. S. 5:10-16; Matt. 10:37).

b. The excellency of Christ is derived from the excellency of His person (17:5; Col. 1:13).

c. When Christ was revealed to Paul, he saw the excellency, the supereminence, the supreme preciousness, of Christ and suffered the loss of all things and counted them as refuse so that he might gain Christ (Gal. 1:15a, 16a; Phil. 3:7-8).

3. "As He reclined at table, a woman came, having an alabaster flask of ointment, of very costly pure nard, and she broke the alabaster flask and poured it over His head" (Mark 14:3):

   a. The gospel causes genuine believers to treasure the Lord Jesus and to value His supreme preciousness (vv. 3-4).

   b. The goal of the gospel is that we would pour out upon the Lord Jesus what is most precious to us, "wasting" ourselves upon Him (Matt. 26:6-8 and footnote on v. 8, Recovery Version).

Day 6   C. We need to appreciate the exceeding worth of the church (13:45-46; Acts 20:28):

   1. "The kingdom of the heavens is like a merchant seeking fine pearls; and finding one pearl of great value, he went and sold all that he had and bought it" (Matt. 13:45-46):

      a. The merchant here is Christ, who was seeking the church for His kingdom.

      b. After finding the church in 16:18 and 18:17, He went to the cross and sold all that He had and bought it for the kingdom.

   2. "Take heed to yourselves and to all the flock, among whom the Holy Spirit has placed you as overseers to shepherd the church of God, which He obtained through His own blood" (Acts 20:28):

      a. *His own blood* indicates the precious love of God for the church and the preciousness, the exceeding worth, of the church as a treasure to God.

      b. Paul's emphasis here is the value of the church as a treasure to God, a treasure that He acquired with His own precious blood (1 John 1:7; 1 Pet. 1:18-19).

      c. The church was precious to Paul because he realized that the desire of the

Lord's heart is to gain the church and that He obtained the church through His own blood; therefore, Paul was willing, most gladly, to spend and be utterly spent for the church (Eph. 1:5, 9; Matt. 16:18; Acts 20:28; 2 Cor. 12:15).

Morning Nourishment

Rev. And He cried with a strong voice, saying, Fallen,
18:2 fallen is Babylon the Great! And she has become a
      dwelling place of demons and a hold of every unclean
      spirit and a hold of every unclean and hateful bird.
2 Pet. Through which He has granted to us precious and
1:4   exceedingly great promises that through these you
      might become partakers of the divine nature, having
      escaped the corruption which is in the world by lust.

Zechariah 5:5-11 describes the vision of the ephah vessel, which is
the measuring vessel, a container able to hold one ephah, used for
purchasing and selling in business....[The angel said to Zecha-
riah], "This is the ephah vessel that goes forth; and he said, This is
their appearance in all the land" (v. 6). A large percentage of the
world's population is engaged in business or commerce. The appearance of business is not that bad; rather, in all the land commerce seems to have a proper appearance. But as we will see, actually today's commerce is totally wicked. (Life-study of Zechariah, p. 35)

Today's Reading

[Zechariah 5:7b-8a says,] "This is a woman sitting within the
ephah vessel. Then he said, This is Wickedness." This reveals that
the woman sitting within the ephah vessel signifies the wickedness contained in commerce, such as covetousness, deceit, and the
love of mammon....The vision in Zechariah 5 corresponds to that of
Babylon the Great in Revelation 18. These visions show us that in
the sight of God the wickedness contained in commerce is a kind
of idolatry and fornication. Business is an adulterous woman de-
sirous of making money. (Life-study of Zechariah, pp. 35-36)

Ezekiel 28 speaks of the king of Tyre, who typifies Satan. He
fell because of the multitude of his merchandise. Merchandising
is a purely commercial activity. Ezekiel 28 is the record of the
first commerce, whereas Revelation 18 is the record of the final
commerce. Ezekiel 28 is the beginning of world commerce,
whereas Revelation 18 is the consummation of world commerce. Revelation 18:11 speaks of "the merchants of the earth."

"Merchants" refers to great entrepreneurs. Antichrist will use Babylon to carry out his commercial activities.

Today our thoughts have to be controlled by God. Those who are for money see nothing but money. They do not see how many fishes have been added; they only see how many dollars have come in. Pure commerce is too great a temptation for man. (*The Collected Works of Watchman Nee,* vol. 57, pp. 182-183)

According to the Bible, God has no intention for a Christian to engage in commerce. I believe all of you are clear that the first case of commerce was with the prince of Tyre. Ezekiel 28:16 says, "By the abundance of your trading they filled your midst with violence, and you sinned." The word *trading* refers to a kind of free commerce....The prince of Tyre was the beginning of profiteering through trade. He was also the beginning of transgression. The prince of Tyre is a type of Satan. When we come to the great Babylon, we find the peak of development in commerce. Babylon's origin is Babel. The most severe judgment from God will be brought against Babylon because it will be the consummation of aggrandizement by trade and the epitome of sin. Revelation 13 speaks of the mark of the beast. Without the mark no one can trade (vv. 16-17). Hence, if pure commerce disappears, the mark of the beast will become useless. The more highly developed commerce becomes, the more useful the mark of the beast will be.

Because some brothers cannot find the right occupation in the church, [working with their own hands, producing and manufacturing by their own labor,] they are forced to engage in pure commerce in the secular business world. Sometimes they are forced to lie and cheat. Soon their hearts become corrupted. In the future we have to do our best to help the brothers make the right choice; we have to show them the clear way. Perhaps some brothers should start some businesses and hire some brothers to work for them. (*The Collected Works of Watchman Nee,* vol. 61, pp. 162-163)

Further Reading: Life-study of Zechariah, msg. 6; The Collected Works of Watchman Nee, vol. 57, ch. 16; vol. 49, ch. 28

Enlightenment and inspiration: _____

_____

_____

_____

Morning Nourishment

Matt. **Then Peter answered and said to Him, Behold, we**
19:27 **have left all and followed You. What then will there**
be for us?

In Zechariah 5:7 and 8 we see that a lead cover, a lead weight, is thrown over the opening of the ephah vessel. This signifies the restriction of the wickedness in commerce by God's sovereignty. Wickedness is hidden and concealed in international trade. If commerce, especially international trade, could be restricted, the whole earth would be holy. (*Life-study of Zechariah*, p. 36)

Today's Reading

[Zechariah 5:9 says,] "Then I lifted up my eyes and I looked, and there were two women going forth." The one woman becoming two women signifies the double effect of commerce once it becomes free of the restriction....The two women had wings like the wings of a stork, and the wind was in their wings. They lifted up the ephah vessel between the earth and the heavens (v. 9b). All this signifies the rapid spreading of the wicked commerce. [Verses 10 and 11 say,] "I said to the angel who spoke with me, Where are they taking the ephah vessel? And he said to me, To build a house for her in the land of Shinar; and when it is prepared, she will be set there in her own place." This signifies that God's sovereignty will cause the wickedness in business, which the people of Israel learned of the Babylonians in their captivity, to go back to Babylon (the land of Shinar). Let this wickedness return to Babylon. All the people among God's elect should be honest and simple in their living. (*Life-study of Zechariah*, pp. 36-37)

Satan's evil concept concerning God's dealing with His seeking people is based on his commercial principle of gain or loss. Satan is a businessman, a merchant (Ezek. 28:16, 18; cf. Rev. 18:11-19), and his thought is according to his commercial principle. He does not recognize that God's purpose in dealing with those who love Him is that they may gain Him to the fullest extent, surpassing the loss of all that they have other than Him (Phil. 3:7-8), that He might be expressed through them for the fulfillment of His purpose in creating man (Gen. 1:26). (Job 1:9, footnote 1)

The parable in Matthew 20:1-16, which is an explanation of the Lord's word to Peter in 19:28-30, concerns the kingdom reward. Peter thought that he was able to pay the price of buying the kingdom, but the Lord indicated to him that the kingdom is priceless and cannot be purchased. Because the kingdom is of peerless worth, we cannot buy it. What the Lord had asked Peter to give up was not the price of gaining the kingdom. He had simply asked Peter to give up all entanglements and frustrations. The kingdom is not a recompense; it is a reward. Peter needed to realize that, having forsaken every entanglement and frustration, he would receive the kingdom as a reward, not as a recompense. This means that the Lord does not act according to the commercial principle, which says that the more we pay, the more we receive. The full enjoyment of eternal life in the manifestation of the kingdom is priceless. (*The Conclusion of the New Testament,* p. 731)

We should not have a commercial mind. Salvation is based upon grace. The Lord Jesus has done everything for us, and there is no need for us to work. The kingdom reward, however, is according to our work, according to the price we pay. If we pay the price, then the Lord will give us a reward. It may seem that the reward is purchased by our work. If we think this, then we are like Peter with a commercial mentality. We need to be reeducated to see that even the reward is based upon grace. The way to receive the reward is not to pay the price, but to enjoy grace. To be saved is to receive grace, and to gain the reward is to enjoy the grace we have received. (*Life-study of Matthew,* pp. 645-646)

[Matthew 20:14] was a strong answer to Peter from the Lord, indicating that the Lord had given him what he thought he deserved. But the Lord has the right to give the same wages to the last workmen according to His own wish, in the principle not of work but of grace. This shattered Peter's natural and commercial mind and corrected his concept. (Matt. 20:14, footnote 1)

Further Reading: Life-study of Matthew, msg. 54; *The Kingdom,* msg. 28

Enlightenment and inspiration: _____

_____

_____

_____

Morning Nourishment

Luke | No household servant can serve two masters; for
16:13 | either he will hate the one and love the other, or he
will hold to one and despise the other. You cannot
serve God and mammon.

Heb. | Let your way of life be without the love of money,
13:5 | being satisfied with the things which are at hand;
for He Himself has said, "I shall by no means give
you up, neither by any means shall I abandon you."

In [Luke 16:13] the Greek word for "serve" means "serve as a slave." Here the Lord indicates that to serve Him requires us to love Him, giving our hearts to Him, and cleave to Him, giving our entire being to Him. Thus we are released from the occupation and usurpation of mammon so that we may serve the Lord wholly and fully. The Lord emphasizes here that to serve Him we must overcome the enticing deceitful mammon of unrighteousness.

In verse 13 we see that mammon is in rivalry with God, competing with Him. Because mammon is in rivalry with God, it is evil. On our part, we cannot serve two lords. We serve either God or mammon. This matter is very serious. (*Life-study of Luke*, p. 309)

Today's Reading

Matthew 6:24 says, "No one can serve two masters, for either he will hate the one and love the other, or he will hold to one and despise the other. You cannot serve God and mammon." The word mammon is an Aramaic word signifying wealth, riches. Here mammon, standing in opposition to God, indicates that wealth or riches is the opponent of God, robbing God's people of their service to Him. (*Life-study of Matthew*, p. 272)

If we are truly under God's administration in resurrection, we shall overcome money and material possessions. They will have no power over us, and they will not occupy us or possess us. Instead, we shall overcome them and reign over them.

In 1 Corinthians 15 Paul deals with the matter of resurrection. Then he opens chapter 16 with a word about collecting material gifts on the first day of the week. The first day of the week signifies resurrection, for it is the day of resurrection. The fact that material things are offered on the first day of the week indicates that they should be presented in resurrection, not in our natural life. Certain wealthy worldly people are able to write checks for large sums of money. But if they make a large donation, they usually make a name for themselves and advertise what they have done. This is not giving in resurrection. Our giving of money and material things must be in resurrection. This way of giving is a strong indication that we are under God's administration in resurrection and have overcome the possession of material things. As a result, God's administration will have a way to be carried on among us. (*Life-study of 1 Corinthians,* pp. 465-466)

Whatever one loves, his whole heart, even his entire being, is set on and occupied and possessed by. This is crucial! Whether there would be a day of glory in the church's victory or grievous days of the church's decline depends altogether on what kind of lovers we are. (2 Tim. 3:2, footnote 2)

The Lord Jesus said, "Blessed are the poor in spirit" (Matt. 5:3), but many people are not poor in spirit. They crave mammon. They crave it because they do not have it. This proves that they have not been delivered from the power of mammon. In 1 Timothy 6:9-10 Paul said that those who intend to be rich and aspire after money have pierced themselves through with many pains. This word shows that those who desire to be rich are under the power of mammon. Today I hope that we all will advance step by step and be totally free from the power of mammon. We have to hate mammon as much as we hate sin....We should be like the apostle Peter who said, "Silver and gold I do not possess, but what I have, this I give to you..." (Acts 3:6). The early church did not have silver or gold; it only had the name of the Lord Jesus. Today we have to go back to the very condition at the beginning. (*The Collected Works of Watchman Nee,* vol. 61, pp. 80-81)

Further Reading: Life-study of Luke, msg. 36; *The Collected Works of Watchman Nee,* vol. 57, pp. 155-164

Enlightenment and inspiration: _____

_____

_____

_____

Morning Nourishment

Luke ...The Lord answered and said to her, Martha, Martha,
10:41-42 you are anxious and troubled about many things; but
there is need of one thing, for Mary has chosen the
good part, which shall not be taken away from her.

Before a person believes in the Lord, his concept of value is
perverted. But once a person is saved, his concept of value
changes. He no longer cherishes what he once cherished, and
he treasures what he once despised. This is a change in his concept of value. Anyone who has not witnessed such a change in
concept is not a genuine Christian....The Bible has much to say
concerning a change in one's concept of value. Such passages on
this change can shed light to the new believers. These passages
show us the *proper* concept of value for a Christian. (*The Collected Works of Watchman Nee,* vol. 60, pp. 387-388)

Today's Reading

Psalm 118:22 says, "The stone which the builders rejected / Has
become the head of the corner."...God treasured the cornerstone
which was rejected by the Jewish builders and used it for the building of His salvation. How different are these two kinds of valuation!
We have to bring new believers to such a change in valuation....We
have to show them that what was once worthless is now priceless.

Hebrews 11:24-26 speaks of a change in concept of enjoyment and suffering. Moses saw the difference. He saw that all
the enjoyment of Egypt was but enjoyment of sin. He considered
it great riches to suffer together with the people of God. He was
well qualified to have the enjoyment of sin because he was the
son of Pharaoh's daughter, the richest and most powerful person
on earth. Yet he refused to be called the son of Pharaoh's daughter, considering the reproach of the Christ greater riches than
the treasures of Egypt. He was very clear about this change in
valuation. He was willing to suffer all reproaches and hardships
because he saw the significance of that unseen, great reward.

Philippians 3:7-8 says, "But what things were gains to me,
these I have counted as loss on account of Christ. But moreover I

also count all things to be loss on account of the excellency of the knowledge of Christ Jesus my Lord, on account of whom I have suffered the loss of all things and count them as refuse that I may gain Christ." Here we see that Paul also had a change in his concept of value. What things were gains to him, these he counted as loss on account of Christ. Why was Paul able to reject the things that were gains to him? He was able to consider them as loss on account of the excellency of the knowledge of Christ Jesus. He reckoned the Christ whom God had anointed as Lord, as King, and as the most excellent One. For His sake he suffered the loss of all things and counted them as refuse. This is the kind of change in valuation that happens to a Christian.

Finally, we want to conclude with the words of Jeremiah 15:19 which tell us that if we bring out the precious from the worthless, we will be as God's mouth. If we cannot tell the proper value of things, God will reject us and cast us aside. He requires that we bring out the precious from the worthless so that we can be His mouth. We have to see the importance of such a change in concept of value. May the Lord grant us the light to have a thorough change in our concept of value so that we will know to choose the most excellent portion. (*The Collected Works of Watchman Nee,* vol. 60, pp. 388, 394-395)

In 1 Peter 2:7 Peter goes on to say, "To you therefore who believe is the preciousness; but to the unbelieving, 'The stone which the builders rejected, this has become the head of the corner.'" In Greek, the word rendered "preciousness" here is a kindred word to honor in verses 4 and 6. The very Christ chosen by God as a stone, even a cornerstone held in honor, is the preciousness to His believers. But to the unbelieving, He is a rejected, despised stone. Christ's preciousness is not only a matter of condition, but also a matter of His position. For Him to be precious means that He is held in honor, that He occupies an honorable position. (*Life-study of 1 Peter,* p. 144)

Further Reading: The Collected Works of Watchman Nee, vol. 60, ch. 45; *Messages Given to the Working Saints,* ch. 7

Enlightenment and inspiration: _____

_____

_____

_____

Morning Nourishment

Phil.   ...What things were gains to me, these I have counted
3:7-8   as loss on account of Christ. But moreover I also
        count all things to be loss on account of the excel-
        lency of the knowledge of Christ Jesus my Lord, on
        account of whom I have suffered the loss of all things
        and count *them* as refuse that I may gain Christ.

The excellency of the knowledge of Christ is derived from the excellency of His person. The Jews consider the law of God given through Moses the most excellent thing in human history; hence, they are zealous for the law. Paul participated in that zeal. But when Christ was revealed to him by God (Gal. 1:15-16), he saw that the excellency, the supereminence, the supreme preciousness, the surpassing worth, of Christ far exceeded the excellency of the law. His knowledge of Christ issued in the excellency of the knowledge of Christ. Since Christ is excellent, the knowledge of Christ is also excellent. On account of this, he counted as loss not only the law and the religion founded according to the law but all things. Like Paul, we should have the knowledge of Christ in His excellency. We should count all things to be loss on account of the excellent knowledge of Christ. (*The Conclusion of the New Testament,* pp. 3499-3500)

Today's Reading

In Philippians 3:7 Paul says, "On account of Christ," but in verse 8 he goes further and says, "On account of the excellency of the knowledge of Christ Jesus my Lord." The addition of the words *my Lord* indicates that as Paul was writing, he was filled with intimate, tender feelings concerning Christ. Tender feelings concerning the preciousness of the Lord Jesus rose up within him, causing him to speak of "Christ Jesus my Lord." Paul placed great value on the excellency of the knowledge of his dear Lord Jesus Christ.

The excellency of the knowledge of Christ is mentioned in verse 8, whereas the actual experience of Christ is implied in verse 10....By knowledge we actually mean a revelation, a vision, concerning Christ and His excellence. The excellency of the knowledge of Christ is the excellency of Christ realized by us. If we lack the knowledge of Christ's excellency, His excellency will not mean anything to us. Christ is unlimited; hence, we need to have the excellency of the knowledge of the unlimited Christ, that is, to have a vision of the preciousness of Christ. When Paul was blind and in religion, he could not see Christ; he could see only the law. Thus, he had the excellency of the knowledge of the law. But after Christ was revealed to him, he began to have the excellency of the knowledge of Christ. He was captured by the excellency of knowing Christ, and for the sake of this knowledge, he was willing to drop all things and count them to be loss. If we have more of the excellency of the knowledge of Christ, we will drop everything religious and everything natural on account of Him and on account of the excellency of the knowledge of Him. (*The Conclusion of the New Testament,* pp. 3500-3501)

We urgently need the excellent knowledge of Christ. Paul was so desperate to have the excellency of the knowledge of Christ that he was willing to count all things loss on account of this knowledge....We need a revelation of Christ's excellency, of His supreme preciousness. (*Life-study of Philippians,* p. 161)

[In Matthew 26:8] the disciples considered Mary's love offering to the Lord a waste. Throughout the past twenty centuries thousands of precious lives, heart treasures, high positions, and golden futures have been "wasted" upon the Lord Jesus. To those who love Him in such a way He is altogether lovely and worthy of their offering. What they have poured upon Him is not a waste but a fragrant testimony of His sweetness. (Matt. 26:8, footnote 1)

Mary received the revelation of the Lord's death through the Lord's words in 16:21; 17:22-23; 20:18-19; and 26:2. Hence, she grasped the opportunity to pour upon the Lord the best that she had. To love the Lord with our best requires a revelation concerning Him. (Matt. 26:12, footnote 1)

Further Reading: The Conclusion of the New Testament, msg. 348;
The Collected Works of Watchman Nee, vol. 21, pp. 5-17

Enlightenment and inspiration: _____

_____

_____

_____

Morning Nourishment

Matt. Again, the kingdom of the heavens is like a merchant
13:45-46 seeking fine pearls; and finding one pearl of great
value, he went and sold all that he had and bought it.
Acts Take heed to yourselves and to all the flock, among
20:28 whom the Holy Spirit has placed you as overseers
to shepherd the church of God, which He obtained
through His own blood.

The merchant in Matthew 13:45 is also Christ, who was
seeking the church for His kingdom. After finding it in 16:18
and 18:17, He went to the cross and sold all He had and bought
it for the kingdom.

In 13:46 we see the heavenly King's work in gaining the one
pearl of great value. At the cross He sold all, whatever He had,
and bought that pearl. The pearl, produced in the death waters
(the world filled with death) by the living oyster (the living
Christ), wounded by a little rock (the sinner) and secreting its life-
juice around the wounding rock (the believer), is also the material
for the building of the New Jerusalem. Since the pearl comes out
of the sea, which signifies the world corrupted by Satan (Isa.
57:20; Rev. 17:15), it must refer to the church, which is mainly constituted with regenerated believers from the Gentile world, and
which is of great value. (*Life-study of Matthew*, p. 478)

Today's Reading

The Lord is not only seeking the kingdom; He also desires a
beautiful church, the pearl. We have pointed out that, according to Revelation 21, the New Jerusalem is built with precious
stones and pearls. In other words, the New Jerusalem is a com-
bination of the treasure and the pearl.…Ultimately, in the New
Jerusalem the kingdom and the church become one entity.
(*Life-study of Matthew*, p. 479)

Let us read Acts 20:28 again: "Take heed to yourselves and to
all the flock, among whom the Holy Spirit has placed you as
overseers to shepherd the church of God, which He obtained

through His own blood." Here, in his charge to the elders of the church in Ephesus, Paul speaks both of the Holy Spirit and of God's own blood in order to indicate his feeling concerning the preciousness of the church. According to Paul's understanding, the church is altogether precious. The church is under the care of the Holy Spirit, and the church has been bought by God with His own blood. Hence, the church is a treasure in the sight of God. Paul treasured the church even as God does.

In 20:28 Paul charged the elders to treasure the church as God does and he did. The fact that God purchased the church with His own blood indicates the preciousness of the church in His sight. Having paid such a price for the church, the church surely is dear to Him. Moreover, the church is under the care of the Holy Spirit. According to Paul's word in verse 28, the elders should consider the church very precious, regarding it as a treasure in the sight of God. The elders, in shepherding the church, should have the same feeling about the church that God has. (*Life-study of Acts,* pp. 473-474)

[Acts 20:28 indicates] the precious love of God for the church and the preciousness, the exceeding worth, of the church in the eyes of God. Here the apostle did not touch the divine life and nature of the church as in Ephesians 5:23-32, but the value of the church as a treasure to God, a treasure which He acquired with His own precious blood....Both the Holy Spirit and God's own blood are divine provisions for the church that He treasures. The Holy Spirit is God Himself, and God's own blood denotes God's work. God's redemptive work acquired the church; now God Himself, the all-inclusive life-giving Spirit (1 Cor. 15:45), cares for the church through the overseers. (Acts 20:28, footnote 5)

The apostle did not care for his own life, but he was very concerned for the future of the church, which was a treasure to him as well as to God. (Acts 20:29, footnote 1)

Further Reading: Life-study of Matthew, msg. 39; *Life-study of Acts,* msg. 54

Enlightenment and inspiration: _____

_____

_____

_____

Hymns, #1153

1 We have found the Christ who's all in all;
 He is everything to us;
 O how blest upon His name to call,
 How divine, how glorious!

   It is joy unspeakable and full of glory,
    Full of glory, full of glory;
   It is joy unspeakable and full of glory,
    And the half has never yet been told!

2 We have found that Christ the Spirit is
 Who within our spirit dwells;
 How available, how near He is,
 And His sweetness all excels.

3 We have found the way to live by Christ —
 Pray His Word and call His name!
 This — the eating, drinking — has sufficed
 And its worth we now proclaim.

4 We have found the local church, our home;
 We are home and home indeed!
 Nevermore in Babylon we roam;
 In the church is all we need.

5 We have found that meeting with the saints
 Is the greatest joy on earth;
 'Tis by this our spirit never faints
 And our lives are filled with worth.

Composition for prophecy with main point and sub-points: _____

_____

_____

_____

_____

_____

_____

_____

_____

_____

_____

_____

_____

_____

_____

_____

_____

_____

_____

_____

_____

_____

_____

_____

_____

_____

_____

_____

_____

_____

_____

_____

_____

_____

_____

_____

The Priesthood and the Kingship
for the Building Up of the Church
as the Temple of God

Scripture Reading: Zech. 6:11-15; Gen. 1:26; 1 Pet. 2:5, 9;
Heb. 4:16; Rev. 22:1

Day 1   I. **The visions in Zechariah of comfort, conso-**
lation, and encouragement are confirmed
by the crowning of Joshua the high priest—
typifying Christ in His priesthood—linked
with Zerubbabel the governor of Judah—
typifying Christ as the Shoot of David in His
kingship (6:11-15):

A. Christ is the Shoot of Jehovah, referring to His divinity; *the Shoot of Jehovah* denotes that through
His incarnation Christ is a new development of
Jehovah God for the Triune God to branch Himself out in His divinity into humanity; this is for
Jehovah God's increase and spread in the universe (Isa. 4:2; 7:14; Matt. 1:22-23).

B. Christ is also the Shoot of David (typified by
Zerubbabel), referring to His humanity and royal
faithfulness (Zech. 3:8; Jer. 23:5).

C. Christ, typified in Zechariah 6:11-13 by two persons, Joshua and Zerubbabel, is the unique One
to hold the two offices of the priesthood and the
kingship.

D. "The counsel of peace will be between the two of
them" (v. 13b); *between the two* means between
the priesthood and the kingship (cf. 1:1; Ezra
5:1).

Day 2   II. **The focus of Hebrews is the heavenly Christ,**
and the main point of the heavenly Christ is
that He is both the High Priest and the King
(the King of righteousness and the King of
peace), as typified by Melchizedek (5:10; 7:1-3,
28; 8:1-2):

A. Christ is not only the King with power and authority but also the High Priest according to the order of Melchizedek (2:17; 4:14; 5:6, 10; 6:20; 8:1; 9:11; Psa. 110:1-4):

1. Christ's heavenly ministry in His ascension includes both His kingship and His priesthood for the building up of the church as the temple of Jehovah, the temple of God (Heb. 7:1-2; Zech. 6:13, 15; 1 Cor. 3:16-17).

2. As the King He has the scepter to rule over the earth and to manage our affairs, and as the High Priest He is interceding for us and taking care of our case before God (Heb. 4:14-16; 7:25-26; 9:24; Rom. 8:34; Rev. 1:12-13).

B. As the kingly High Priest according to the order of Melchizedek, Christ ministers God into us as our supply to fulfill God's eternal purpose (Heb. 7:1-2; 8:1-2; Gen. 14:18-20):

1. In His earthly ministry Christ was a High Priest according to the order of Aaron for the putting away of sin (Heb. 9:14, 26).

2. Then, in His heavenly ministry Christ was designated a High Priest according to the order of Melchizedek (5:6, 10), not to offer sacrifices for sin but to minister to us the very God who was processed through incarnation, human living, crucifixion, and resurrection, signified by the bread and the wine (Matt. 26:26-28), as our life supply to nourish, refresh, sustain, comfort, and strengthen us so that we may be saved to the uttermost (Heb. 7:25).

Day 3

C. Christ's kingly priesthood is for fighting against God's enemies to bring in righteousness and peace so that He may minister the processed Triune God into us as our daily supply and enjoyment (vv. 1-2; Gen. 14:18-20).

D. Christ's divine priesthood is for saving us to the uttermost in His life unto glorification from all the by-products of death, such as vanity, groaning, sighing, decay, bondage, corruption, and slavery; His divine priesthood is the absence of death and the presence of life (Heb. 7:25, 28; Rom. 5:10; 8:19, 21, 23, 30).

Day 4 III. **The priesthood and the kingship are for God's image and dominion; the priesthood causes man to have the image of God, and the kingship causes man to have the dominion of God to accomplish God's original intention:**

A. There are two main aspects in the creation of man: image and dominion (Gen. 1:26); image refers to the expression of God, and dominion is for the representation of God to deal with His enemy.

B. The priesthood is for the expression of God; the priests enjoy the Lord, and they become His expression, manifestation, habitation, and dwelling place (His spiritual house as His holy priesthood) (1 Pet. 2:5):

1. The line of "image" is the line of the priesthood, because only when man draws near to God and allows God to flow through him can God be expressed in His image.

2. The priesthood is for contacting God to be mingled with God and to be transformed into and conformed to Christ's image for His expression (2 Cor. 3:18; Rom. 8:28-29).

C. The kingship is for the Lord's authority, His dominion; the kings represent God with His authority to deal with His enemy (Matt. 28:19-20; Rom. 16:20):

1. The line of "dominion" is the line of the kingship, because a king receives authority from God in order to reign for God.

2. The kingship is for reigning in life (by the abundance of grace and the inward reigning of grace) over Satan, sin, and death to represent God with His dominion for His kingdom (5:17, 21).

D. The redemption accomplished through Christ's blood "made us a kingdom, priests to His God and Father" (Rev. 1:5b-6a).

E. In the millennium the overcomers will be priests, drawing near to God and Christ, and they will also be kings, reigning over the nations with Christ (2:26-27; 20:4, 6).

F. The believers who are defeated will forfeit this reward; however, after being dealt with in the millennium, these defeated ones will participate in the blessing of this reward in that they will serve God in the priesthood and represent God in the kingship as the New Jerusalem in the new heaven and new earth (22:3, 5):

1. When the New Jerusalem is manifested, the holy city is like jasper (21:11, 18a); jasper denotes the image of God, because God's appearance is like jasper (4:3); in the holy city the water of life—the Spirit of life—flows to fill the city with God; hence, the image of God, the expression of God, is fully realized.

2. Furthermore, those who are a part of the New Jerusalem will reign as kings and exercise God's authority for eternity (22:5).

Day 5 IV. **The throne and the river of water of life in Revelation 22:1 speak of Christ being both the King and the Priest:**

A. According to the picture of the New Jerusalem, the authority of the throne and the fellowship of life, the flow of life (v. 1), are for the building of the New Jerusalem; this corresponds to Zechariah 6:12-13, which speaks of the offices of the priesthood and the kingship converging in Joshua and Zerubbabel, who are types of the Lord Jesus, for the sake of the building of God's temple:

1. The river of water of life, the flow of life, is the divine fellowship of being saturated and soaked with God for His holy priesthood with His image, His expression (1 Pet. 2:5).

2. The throne of God and of the Lamb is the rule and headship of Christ as the embodiment of God for His royal priesthood with His dominion, His kingdom (v. 9).

B. The priests draw near to God, enter into the Holy of Holies to touch the throne of God, and allow God as rivers of living water to flow through them and into other persons (John 7:37-39a); the flowing of the water of life from the throne is the only way that builds up the church of God.

C. In Hebrews Christ as the Priest brings the believers into the Holy of Holies, that is, into fellowship with God (2:17; 3:1; 4:14; 5:6; 7:1); in Matthew Christ as the King is Emmanuel, God with us, the One who joins God with man and brings the authority of God to man (1:1, 23; 2:6):

1. Hebrews speaks of the building of a city (11:9-10, 16; 12:22), whereas the Gospel of Matthew speaks of the building of the church (16:18); the building of the church and the building of the city are the same thing.

2. Christ is both the Priest and the King for God's building; in Christ there is the fellowship of the priesthood and the authority of the kingship, both of which are for God's building; on the one hand, Christ flows out the fellowship of life to us for God's image, and on the other hand, He brings us under the authority of the throne for God's dominion.

D. First Peter 2:9 reveals that the redeemed ones are a "royal priesthood"; the word *royal* means that we have the position and authority of a king (the throne), and the word *priesthood* indicates that we have the fellowship of life (the river of water of life).

E. Everyone among us should be a royal priest (v. 9), one who has the flow of life from the throne; in every one of us there should be an expression of both the priesthood and the kingship; God's intention for His people is to make them a kingdom of priests (Exo. 19:4, 6; Rev. 5:10).

Day 6   V. **According to Hebrews 4:16, the way to minister as a priest is simply to come forward to the throne of grace to receive mercy and find grace for timely help:**

A. We should compare Hebrews 4:16 with Revelation 22:1, which says that the river of water of life proceeds out of the throne of God.

B. When we come forward to behold God and contact Him by praying in our spirit to touch His throne, we experience the Spirit flowing in us, flowing through us, and supplying us.

C. This supply, this flow of the Spirit of life, is the timely help, which is the mercy and grace of God; mercy and grace refer to God flowing through us and being gained by us.

D. Timely help is the living God, the flowing God, coming into us and flowing through us to refresh, water, and supply us; whenever, by the Lord's blood (Heb. 10:19-20), we come forward and touch the throne of grace, God flows to refresh and water us, and we experience indescribable joy, no matter how harsh the circumstances are (1 Pet. 1:8).

E. To the believers this throne is the throne of grace, but to God's enemy it is the throne of authority; the throne of grace is related to the priesthood, and the throne of authority is related to the kingship:

   1. Out from the throne of God flows the river of water of life for grace (Rev. 22:1) and the river of fire for judgment (Dan. 7:9-10).

   2. The flow of the river of water of life produces the New Jerusalem as a city of water, but the river of the fire of God's judgment flows into the lake of fire.

   3. When we touch the throne of grace and allow the water of life to flow through us,

we receive mercy and grace for timely help; then we can touch His throne of authority so that He can judge the improper situations within us.

F. God wants us to enter into the Holy of Holies, our spirit, in order to touch the throne of grace and allow the water of life to flow through us; this flow will bring us into the fellowship with God and will cause us to be built up in His life to be His dwelling place, His spiritual house, His holy and royal priesthood (1 Pet. 2:5, 9).

Morning Nourishment

Zech. ...Thus speaks Jehovah of hosts, saying, Here is a man,
6:12-13 whose name is the Shoot; and he will shoot forth from
his place and will build the temple of Jehovah. Indeed, it is he who will build the temple of Jehovah;
and he will bear majesty and will sit and rule on his
throne; and he will be a priest on his throne; and the
counsel of peace will be between the two of them.

The previous eight visions [in Zechariah] of comfort, conso-
lation, and encouragement are confirmed by the crowning of
Joshua the high priest—typifying Christ in His priesthood—
linked with Zerubbabel the governor of Judah (6:12-13), typifying Christ as the Shoot of David in His kingship (see footnotes
1^1 and 8^1 in ch. 3).Christ, typified in 6:11-13 by two persons,
Joshua and Zerubbabel, is the unique One to hold the two
offices of the priesthood and the kingship. In all history He is
the only person qualified to bear the responsibilities of these
two offices in God's administration. Thus, in Hebrews 7 Christ
is both the High Priest and the King, as typified by Melchizedek (cf. Gen. 14:18). Because Melchizedek bore the two offices
of the priesthood and the kingship, he was a type of Christ as
the One who would bear both the priesthood and the kingship
in God's administration. (Zech. 6:11, footnote 1)

Today's Reading

In Isaiah Christ is unveiled as the God-man. *The Shoot of
Jehovah* refers to Christ's deity, showing His divine nature, and
the fruit of the earth (Luke 1:42) refers to Christ's humanity with
His human nature. As the Shoot of Jehovah, Christ comes out of
God, out of eternity (John 8:42; Micah 5:2). As the fruit of the
earth, Christ, having a human body made of dust (Gen. 2:7),
grows out of the earth (cf. Isa. 53:2)....*The Shoot of Jehovah*
denotes that through His incarnation Christ is a new development of Jehovah God for the Triune God to branch Himself out in
His divinity into humanity (7:14; Matt. 1:22-23). This is for Jehovah God's increase and spread in the universe. *The fruit of the*

earth denotes that Christ, as the divine Shoot of Jehovah, also becomes a man of flesh from the earth (John 1:14; Heb. 2:14). This is for the Triune God to be multiplied and reproduced in humanity. As a man with the divine life, He is a seed, a grain of wheat, to produce many grains, His believers as His many brothers, through His death and resurrection (John 12:24; 20:17; Rom. 8:29).

The Shoot of Jehovah denotes the riches, the refreshing, the vigor, the growth, and the productive power of the divine life. *The fruit of the earth* denotes the produce brought forth, carried out, and expressed in Christ's humanity. As seen in the four Gospels, all the fruit born by Christ came out of the divine life, but it was produced in Christ's humanity. (Isa. 4:2, footnote 2)

[In Zechariah 3:8 *My servant, the shoot*] refers to Zerubbabel, who is a type of Christ as the Servant of Jehovah, the Shoot of David (Jer. 23:5), in His humanity and royal faithfulness (Zech. 6:12). Although he was not a king but was a governor in the position of a king (Hag. 1:1), Zerubbabel was nevertheless a descendant, a shoot, of the royal family of David. As such, he typifies Christ. (Zech. 3:8, footnote 1)

[In Zechariah 6:13] *between the two* means between the priesthood and the kingship. In the Old Testament no king could be a priest, but in the millennium both Christ and the overcomers will be kings to reign and priests to serve God. These two responsibilities will be reconciled in both Christ and the overcomers. In the millennium the overcomers will be priests, drawing near to God and Christ, and they will also be kings, reigning over the nations with Christ (Rev. 2:26-27; 20:4, 6). This will be a reward to the overcomers. The believers who are defeated in this age will forfeit this reward. However, after being dealt with in the millennium, these defeated ones will participate in the blessing of this reward in that they will serve God in the priesthood and represent God in the kingship in the new heaven and new earth for eternity (Rev. 22:3, 5). (Zech. 6:13, footnote 1)

Further Reading: The Priesthood, ch. 4

Enlightenment and inspiration: _____

_____
_____
_____

Morning Nourishment

Psa. Jehovah has sworn, and He will not change: You are a
110:4 Priest forever according to the order of Melchizedek.
Heb. Now in the things which are being said the chief
8:1-2 point *is this:* We have such a High Priest, who sat
down on the right hand of the throne of the Majesty
in the heavens, a Minister of the holy places, even of
the true tabernacle, which the Lord pitched, not man.

The Christ in heaven who can be experienced by us subjectively
in our spirit is mainly the High Priest. The book of Hebrews is
focused on the heavenly Christ, and the chief point of this
heavenly Christ is that He is the High Priest. The main point here
is not that Christ is the Savior or Redeemer but that He, as the
heavenly Christ, is the High Priest. This is the reason why the book
of Hebrews is primarily concerned with the priesthood of Christ.
Please remember the following statements: the focus of Hebrews
is the heavenly Christ, the main point of the heavenly Christ is
that He is the High Priest, and Hebrews is concerned primarily
with the priesthood of Christ. (*Life-study of Hebrews,* p. 359)

Today's Reading

Christ is not only the King with power and authority (Psa. 110:1-2);
He is also the High Priest (Heb. 2:17; 4:14; 6:20; 8:1; 9:11). Christ's
heavenly ministry in His ascension includes both His kingship
and His priesthood. As the King He has the scepter to rule over
the earth and to manage our affairs, and as the High Priest He is
interceding for us and taking care of our case before God (Heb.
7:25-26; 9:24; Rom. 8:34; Rev. 1:12-13). (Psa. 110:4, footnote 1)

As the High Priest, Christ ministers God Himself and the
riches of the divine life to us. As the God-man, He is more than
fully qualified to be our High Priest. (Heb. 2:17, footnote 2)

The priesthood of Melchizedek is mentioned in the Scriptures
[Gen. 14:18] before the priesthood of Aaron (Exo. 28:1). The
priesthood according to the order of Melchizedek is higher than
the Aaronic priesthood (Heb. 7). In His earthly ministry Christ

was a High Priest according to the order of Aaron for the putting away of sin (Heb. 9:14, 26). Then, in His heavenly ministry Christ was designated a High Priest according to the order of Melchizedek (Heb. 5:6, 10), not to offer sacrifices for sin but to minister to us the very God who was processed through incarnation, human living, crucifixion, and resurrection, signified by the bread and the wine (Matt. 26:26-28), as our life supply that we may be saved to the uttermost (Heb. 7:25a). (Gen. 14:18, footnote 3)

Whenever most Christians speak about Christ as our High Priest, they still cling to the concept that He is the High Priest offering sacrifices to God for our sins. This, of course, is correct. But it is on the negative side. Christ as the High Priest offering sacrifices to God for our sins is typified by Aaron. That was in the past. Today Christ is no longer offering sacrifices for our sins but ministering God to us as our supply. In the past, Christ offered sacrifices to God for our sins as typified by Aaron. Today He is ministering God to us as our supply according to the order of Melchizedek.

This is proved by the coming of Melchizedek to Abraham (Gen. 14:18-22). The first mention of the word priest in the Bible is with Melchizedek. Melchizedek was the priest of the Most High God. As the priest of the Most High God, Melchizedek did not offer sacrifices to God for Abraham's sin; he ministered bread and wine to him. As indicated by the symbols of the Lord's table in the Bible bread and wine signify the processed God as our supply. Our High Priest, Christ, is not according to the order of Aaron offering sacrifices to God; He is according to the order of Melchizedek ministering the processed God to us.

Who are we? We are no longer poor sinners but victorious fighters....When Melchizedek came to him, Abraham was the victor, the fighter, the slaughterer. Abraham had just slaughtered Chedorlaomer and the other kings (Gen. 14:17). Abraham was a victorious fighter who had taken many spoils. (*Life-study of Hebrews,* pp. 359-360)

Further Reading: Life-study of Hebrews, msgs. 32, 35

Enlightenment and inspiration: _____

_____
_____
_____

Morning Nourishment

Heb. ...*It is* according to the likeness of Melchizedek *that* a
7:15-16 different Priest arises, who has been appointed not according to the law of a fleshy commandment but according to the power of an indestructible life.
  25 Hence also He is able to save to the uttermost those who come forward to God through Him, since He lives always to intercede for them.

Hebrews 7, a chapter on the priesthood of Christ, reveals two aspects of Christ's priesthood. The first aspect is the kingly priesthood, and the second aspect is the divine priesthood....His status is kingly, royal. Although He is a High Priest, He did not come out of the tribe of the priests but out of the tribe of the kings—Judah. Kingship is His status and makes Him a kingly priest.

Kingship is related to both righteousness and peace because kingship is a kind of rule and authority. In order to maintain righteousness and peace, we need authority. If Christ is to minister the processed God to us as our bread and wine, there must be an environment that is full of righteousness and peace.... Righteousness and peace come out of His kingship, for when the King is here, no one will fight. Everything will be peaceful. (*Life-study of Hebrews*, p. 367)

Today's Reading

For Christ to be kingly is a matter of status, but for Him to be divine is a matter of constituent, a matter of His having the necessary, basic element that constitutes Him to be such a High Priest....Christ is kingly according to His royal status and divine according to His divine nature. He is kingly because He is a King, and He is divine because He is the Son of God. Christ, the Son of God, not only has kingship but also divinity....His divinity constitutes Him as a High Priest who is living and full of life so that He may be able to continue His priesthood perpetually.

With Christ as the divine High Priest there is no death. He has conquered, subdued, and swallowed death. Why is there no death with our divine High Priest? Because He is life. Christ is divine.

Divinity is His very essence, nature, element, and makeup.... Since Christ is divine, wherever He is, there is no death. Wher-ever He is, there is resurrection and death is swallowed.... Christ's priesthood is the absence of death.

Divinity is the constituent of His priesthood. His priesthood is constituted, composed, with His divinity. As wood is the ele-ment of a table, so divinity is the element of Christ's being the High Priest. When His ministry comes in, it means the absence of death. On the one hand, the priesthood of Christ is the ab-sence of death; on the other hand, it is the presence of life....As the kingly High Priest, Christ ministers the processed God to us, and as the divine High Priest, wherever He is, life is present.... Our High Priest has not been constituted with the law but with the power of an indestructible life [Heb. 7:16].

The Greek word translated uttermost in 7:25 has the same root as the Greek word for perfection....To be saved to the utter-most is to be brought into Christ's perfection. The divine Son of God was incarnated, lived on earth, passed through death, was resurrected, and has been fully perfected forever. This means that in His perfection there is no groaning, vanity, corruption, bond-age, or decay. In Christ, the perfected Son of God, the One who has been resurrected and uplifted, there is no...vanity, groaning, decay, bondage, and corruption [which] are all by-products of death. Christ, the perfected One, is able to save us from all of these by-products of death and to bring us into His perfec-tion....This is the saving to the uttermost, the saving to per-fection. This is the saving of the divine priesthood of Christ.

The life that we have received is an indestructible life, and nothing on earth, in heaven, or in hell can deal with it. This is the life that constitutes the divine priesthood,...[which is why it] is able to save us to the uttermost, saving us from all the by-products of death into Christ's complete perfection—glorifica-tion. (*Life-study of Hebrews,* pp. 368-369, 384, 392)

Further Reading: Life-study of Hebrews, msgs. 33-34

Enlightenment and inspiration: _____

_____

_____

Morning Nourishment

Rev. ...Jesus Christ, the faithful Witness, the Firstborn
1:5-6 of the dead, and the Ruler of the kings of the earth.
To Him who loves us and has released us from our
sins by His blood and made us a kingdom, priests...
20:6 Blessed and holy is he who has part in the first
resurrection;...they will be priests of God and of
Christ and will reign with Him for a thousand years.

God created man in His image so that man would be His
expression, and He gave dominion to man so that man would be
His representation (Gen. 1:26). When the Bible speaks of man, it
first speaks of image and dominion, showing that God cares for
His image and dominion in man....The two lines of the priesthood and the kingship run through the Bible. The priesthood
enables man to express God, and the kingship enables man to
represent God. The priesthood causes man to have the image of
God, and the kingship causes man to have the dominion of God.
(*The Priesthood and God's Building,* pp. 92-93)

Today's Reading

There are two main aspects in the creation of man: image and
authority, dominion (Gen. 1:26). Image refers to the expression of
God, and dominion is for the representation of God to deal with
His enemy. These two aspects were in God's original intention....
He created man with His image that man may be His expression,
and He committed His authority to man that man may be His
representative. From the beginning to the end of the Bible there
are these two lines, the line of image and expression and the line
of dominion and representation.

The priesthood is for the expression of God. The priests enjoy
the Lord, and they become His expression, manifestation, habitation, and dwelling place....The kingship, on the other hand, is for
authority and dominion. The kings represent God to deal with His
enemy. These are the two items of the original intention of God.
(*Functioning in Life as Gifts Given to the Body of Christ,* pp. 78-79)

The line of image is the line of the priesthood, because only when man draws near to God and allows God to flow through him can God's image be expressed. Moses remained in the presence of God and fellowshipped with God for forty days. As a result, he was saturated with God, and his face was shining (Exo. 34:28-30). In those forty days Moses was with God as a priest. He put aside all other matters and remained with God. He lived in the presence of God, touched God, and allowed God to flow through him and saturate him so that his whole being was filled with the glory of God. This shows that those who bear the image of God live the life of a priest in a practical way.

It is easy to associate the line of dominion with the line of the kingship, because a king receives authority from God in order to reign for God. Hence, in the Bible the lines of image and dominion are the lines of the priesthood and the kingship. These two lines run from the beginning of the Bible to the end of the Bible....In the last book of the Bible, Revelation, the apostle John says that the Lord has released us from our sins by His blood so that we might be priests (1:5-6), that the Lord made us priests and a kingdom to reign on the earth (5:10), and that when we are resurrected and enter into glory, we will be priests who will reign with the Lord (20:6). Finally, when the New Jerusalem is manifested, the holy city is like jasper (21:11, 18). Jasper denotes the image of God, because God is like jasper in appearance (4:3). In the holy city the water of life—the Spirit of life—flows to fill the city with God; hence, the image of God is fully expressed. Furthermore, those who are a part of the New Jerusalem will reign as kings and exercise God's authority for eternity (22:5).

God created man with the intention that man would be a priest, that is, a person who draws near to God, allows God to flow through him, is saturated with God, and expresses the glory of God. God also intended that man would exercise His authority. (*The Priesthood and God's Building,* pp. 92-93)

Further Reading: The Priesthood and God's Building, ch. 1; *Functioning in Life as Gifts Given to the Body of Christ,* chs. 7-8

Enlightenment and inspiration: _____

_____

_____

_____

Morning Nourishment

Rev. And he showed me a river of water of life, bright as
22:1 crystal, proceeding out of the throne of God and of
the Lamb in the middle of its street.

1 Pet. But you are a chosen race, a royal priesthood, a holy
2:9 nation, a people acquired for a possession, so that you
may tell out the virtues of Him who has called you out
of darkness into His marvelous light.

[In Revelation 22:1] the throne and the flowing water of life signify authority and fellowship. The throne of God and of the Lamb signifies authority, whereas the flow of the water of life signifies the fellowship of life.

According to the picture in Revelation, the river of water of life flows out of the throne. This, in turn, signifies that the flow of life, the fellowship of life, conveys the authority of the throne.... Authority and fellowship, the two main components of the New Jerusalem, are coordinated. The authority of the throne flows to every part of the city through the fellowship of life; the entire city is in fellowship and under authority. (*The Priesthood and God's Building,* pp. 28-29)

Today's Reading

The throne and the water of life speak of Christ being both the King and the Priest. He came to be the way, the reality, and the life so that the redeemed could have fellowship with God and blend with one another. The water of life points to the aspect of Christ as the Priest. He also brings the authority of the throne to the redeemed. The throne points to the aspect of Christ as the King. The fellowship of life and the authority of the throne are related to the offices of the priesthood and the kingship, both of which belong to the Lord. According to the picture of the New Jerusalem, the authority of the throne and the fellowship of life are for the building of the New Jerusalem. This corresponds to Zechariah 6:12-13, which speaks of the offices of the priesthood and the kingship converging in Joshua, who is a type of the Lord Jesus, for the sake of the building of God's temple.

The book of Hebrews deals particularly with the aspect of

Christ as the Priest,... [showing] that Christ, as the Priest, enables us to enjoy God as our way, our reality, and our life. He brings the believers into the Holy of Holies, that is, into fellowship with God (2:17; 3:1; 4:14; 5:6; 7:1)....The Gospel of Matthew deals particularly with the aspect of Christ as the King, [showing] us that Christ is Emmanuel, joining God with man and bringing the authority of God to man (1:1, 23; 2:6). Although Hebrews speaks of Christ as the Priest and the Gospel of Matthew speaks of Christ as the King, both books speak of the matter of building. Hebrews speaks of the building of a city (11:9-10, 16; 12:22), whereas the Gospel of Mat-thew speaks of the building of the church (16:18). The building of the church and the building of the city are the same thing.

According to the Bible, in addition to Christ, who has the offices of the kingship and the priesthood, the redeemed ones have both offices as well. First Peter 2:9 reveals that the redeemed ones are a "royal priesthood." The word *royal* means that we have the position and authority of a king. The word *priesthood* indicates that we have the fellowship of life....We are joined to Christ, and we have the offices of the kingship and the priesthood. Thus, we are able to meet God's need for the building.

The Lord Jesus is our Priest, and those who receive Him are also priests (1 Pet. 2:5, 9). His priestly life has entered into us; hence, we can draw near to God, fellowship with God, and allow God to flow through us. As believers, we can touch the source of the water of life, and we can allow the water of life to flow into us and to flow out of us as rivers of living water.

The building of the church depends on whether or not the saints will bear the priesthood before God. Only the priests draw near to God, touch the throne of God, and allow God to flow through them. The water of life can flow through them and into other persons. The flowing of the water of life is the only way that builds up the church of God. (*The Priesthood and God's Building*, pp. 31-34, 95, 91)

Further Reading: The Priesthood and God's Building, ch. 2

Enlightenment and inspiration: _____

_____

_____

Morning Nourishment

Heb. Let us therefore come forward with boldness to
4:16 the throne of grace that we may receive mercy and
find grace for timely help.

1 Pet. You yourselves also, as living stones, are being
2:5 built up as a spiritual house into a holy priesthood
to offer up spiritual sacrifices acceptable to God
through Jesus Christ.

According to Hebrews 4:16, the way to minister as a priest is simply to come forward to the throne of grace to receive mercy and find grace for timely help. Revelation 22:1 says that the river of water of life proceeds from the throne of God. If we compare these two verses, we will realize that mercy and grace proceed out of God to be man's life. When we come forward to behold God and contact Him by praying in our spirit and touching His throne, we experience the Spirit flowing in us. The operation of the Spirit in us is not only like the anointing but also like the flowing of the water of life. When we draw near to God in prayer to fellowship with Him, we have an inner sense that the Spirit is flowing through us and supplying us. This supply is the timely help, which is the mercy and grace of God. Although we are unworthy, the mercy of God reaches us and positions us to receive His grace as our timely help. (*The Priesthood and God's Building,* p. 97)

Today's Reading

There are many times when our prayers are not "answered" by God in our way of "timely help."...Whether or not our prayer is "answered," as long as we contact God, He will flow through us as the living water. This flow is our timely help. The problems might remain or even become worse, but inwardly we will experience unspeakable peace and joy. This is timely help. Timely help is the living God, the flowing God, coming into us and flowing through us to refresh, water, and supply us.

The way into the Holy of Holies is now open, and we can enter in (Heb. 10:19-20). We can touch the throne. God and the Lamb are flowing out from the throne to be our supply. Whenever, by the Lord's blood, we come forward and touch the throne of grace, God flows to refresh and water us, and we experience indescribable joy, no matter how harsh the circumstances are.

God has only one throne in the universe. He does not have two thrones. Just as the light is in the lamp, God is in the Lamb. God in Christ is sitting on one throne. To the believers, this throne is the throne of grace, but to God's enemy, it is the throne of authority. The throne of grace is related to the priesthood, and the throne of authority is related to the kingship.

Out from the throne of God flows the river of water of life (Rev. 22:1) and the river of fire (Dan. 7:10). The river of water of life is for grace, and the river of fire is for judgment. Those persons who allow the river of water of life to flow through them will end up in the New Jerusalem, but those who are swept away by the river of fire will end up in the lake of fire. The meaning of the universe is related to these two rivers. The flow of the river of water of life produces a city of water, but the river of the fire of God's judgment flows into the lake of fire.

As believers, we have a twofold status: we are both priests and kings. The priesthood is related to the throne of grace, and the kingship is related to the throne of authority. When we touch the throne of grace and allow the water to flow through us, we receive mercy and grace for timely help. Then we can touch His throne of authority so that He can judge the improper situations within us.

God wants us, His saved ones, to enter into the Holy of Holies in order to touch the throne of grace and allow the water of life to flow through us. Then our inner condition will match the New Jerusalem. The throne of God and of the Lamb will be established in us, and the river of water of life will flow in us. This flow will bring us into fellowship with God and will cause us to be built up in His life to be His holy dwelling place. This is what God desires today. (*The Priesthood and God's Building,* pp. 98-100)

Further Reading: The Priesthood and God's Building, ch. 8

Enlightenment and inspiration: _____

_____

_____

_____

Hymns, #911

1   O how blessed is the priest's life,
    Christ to him is all in all:
    All His clothing, food, and dwelling,
    And His portion therewithal.

    O how blessed is the priest's life,
    Christ to him is all in all:
    All His clothing, food, and dwelling,
    And His portion therewithal.

2   All the clothing of his service
    Is the beauty of the Lord;
    Glorious splendor do his garments,
    Breast and shoulder-piece afford.

3   When in sacrifice he offers
    Christ to God as God has willed,
    Then as food he doth enjoy Him
    And is with His riches filled.

4   Putting on the Lord as clothing,
    Christ without he doth express;
    Eating, drinking, with Him mingled,
    Christ within doth him possess.

5   Holy, glorious is their dwelling,
    'Tis the increase of the Lord;
    Here the priests built up together
    Unto God a house afford.

6   All his portion, all his living,
    Everything the priests possess—
    All is Christ and Christ forever,
    In His all-inclusiveness.

Composition for prophecy with main point and sub-points: _____

Reading Schedule for the Recovery Version of the Old Testament with Footnotes

Wk.	Lord's Day	Monday	Tuesday	Wednesday	Thursday	Friday	Saturday
1	Gen. 1:1-5 ☐	1:6-23 ☐	1:24-31 ☐	2:1-9 ☐	2:10-25 ☐	3:1-13 ☐	3:14-24 ☐
2	4:1-26 ☐	5:1-32 ☐	6:1-22 ☐	7:1—8:3 ☐	8:4-22 ☐	9:1-29 ☐	10:1-32 ☐
3	11:1-32 ☐	12:1-20 ☐	13:1-18 ☐	14:1-24 ☐	15:1-21 ☐	16:1-16 ☐	17:1-27 ☐
4	18:1-33 ☐	19:1-38 ☐	20:1-18 ☐	21:1-34 ☐	22:1-24 ☐	23:1—24:27 ☐	24:28-67 ☐
5	25:1-34 ☐	26:1-35 ☐	27:1-46 ☐	28:1-22 ☐	29:1-35 ☐	30:1-43 ☐	31:1-55 ☐
6	32:1-32 ☐	33:1—34:31 ☐	35:1-29 ☐	36:1-43 ☐	37:1-36 ☐	38:1—39:23 ☐	40:1—41:13 ☐
7	41:14-57 ☐	42:1-38 ☐	43:1-34 ☐	44:1-34 ☐	45:1-28 ☐	46:1-34 ☐	47:1-31 ☐
8	48:1-22 ☐	49:1-15 ☐	49:16-33 ☐	50:1-26 ☐	Exo. 1:1-22 ☐	2:1-25 ☐	3:1-22 ☐
9	4:1-31 ☐	5:1-23 ☐	6:1-30 ☐	7:1-25 ☐	8:1-32 ☐	9:1-35 ☐	10:1-29 ☐
10	11:1-10 ☐	12:1-14 ☐	12:15-36 ☐	12:37-51 ☐	13:1-22 ☐	14:1-31 ☐	15:1-27 ☐
11	16:1-36 ☐	17:1-16 ☐	18:1-27 ☐	19:1-25 ☐	20:1-26 ☐	21:1-36 ☐	22:1-31 ☐
12	23:1-33 ☐	24:1-18 ☐	25:1-22 ☐	25:23-40 ☐	26:1-14 ☐	26:15-37 ☐	27:1-21 ☐
13	28:1-21 ☐	28:22-43 ☐	29:1-21 ☐	29:22-46 ☐	30:1-10 ☐	30:11-38 ☐	31:1-17 ☐
14	31:18—32:35 ☐	33:1-23 ☐	34:1-35 ☐	35:1-35 ☐	36:1-38 ☐	37:1-29 ☐	38:1-31 ☐
15	39:1-43 ☐	40:1-38 ☐	Lev. 1:1-17 ☐	2:1-16 ☐	3:1-17 ☐	4:1-35 ☐	5:1-19 ☐
16	6:1-30 ☐	7:1-38 ☐	8:1-36 ☐	9:1-24 ☐	10:1-20 ☐	11:1-47 ☐	12:1-8 ☐
17	13:1-28 ☐	13:29-59 ☐	14:1-18 ☐	14:19-32 ☐	14:33-57 ☐	15:1-33 ☐	16:1-17 ☐
18	16:18-34 ☐	17:1-16 ☐	18:1-30 ☐	19:1-37 ☐	20:1-27 ☐	21:1-24 ☐	22:1-33 ☐
19	23:1-22 ☐	23:23-44 ☐	24:1-23 ☐	25:1-23 ☐	25:24-55 ☐	26:1-24 ☐	26:25-46 ☐
20	27:1-34 ☐	Num. 1:1-54 ☐	2:1-34 ☐	3:1-51 ☐	4:1-49 ☐	5:1-31 ☐	6:1-27 ☐
21	7:1-41 ☐	7:42-88 ☐	7:89—8:26 ☐	9:1-23 ☐	10:1-36 ☐	11:1-35 ☐	12:1—13:33 ☐
22	14:1-45 ☐	15:1-41 ☐	16:1-50 ☐	17:1—18:7 ☐	18:8-32 ☐	19:1-22 ☐	20:1-29 ☐
23	21:1-35 ☐	22:1-41 ☐	23:1-30 ☐	24:1-25 ☐	25:1-18 ☐	26:1-65 ☐	27:1-23 ☐
24	28:1-31 ☐	29:1-40 ☐	30:1—31:24 ☐	31:25-54 ☐	32:1-42 ☐	33:1-56 ☐	34:1-29 ☐
25	35:1-34 ☐	36:1-13 ☐	Deut. 1:1-46 ☐	2:1-37 ☐	3:1-29 ☐	4:1-49 ☐	5:1-33 ☐
26	6:1—7:26 ☐	8:1-20 ☐	9:1-29 ☐	10:1-22 ☐	11:1-32 ☐	12:1-32 ☐	13:1—14:21 ☐

Reading Schedule for the Recovery Version of the Old Testament with Footnotes

Wk.	Lord's Day	Monday	Tuesday	Wednesday	Thursday	Friday	Saturday
27	☐ 14:22—15:23	☐ 16:1-22	☐ 17:1—18:8	☐ 18:9—19:21	☐ 20:1—21:17	☐ 21:18—22:30	☐ 23:1-25
28	☐ 24:1-22	☐ 25:1-19	☐ 26:1-19	☐ 27:1-26	☐ 28:1-68	☐ 29:1-29	☐ 30:1—31:29
29	☐ 31:30—32:52	☐ 33:1-29	☐ 34:1-12	☐ Josh. 1:1-18	☐ 2:1-24	☐ 3:1-17	☐ 4:1-24
30	☐ 5:1-15	☐ 6:1-27	☐ 7:1-26	☐ 8:1-35	☐ 9:1-27	☐ 10:1-43	☐ 11:1—12:24
31	☐ 13:1-33	☐ 14:1—15:63	☐ 16:1—18:28	☐ 19:1-51	☐ 20:1—21:45	☐ 22:1-34	☐ 23:1—24:33
32	☐ Judg. 1:1-36	☐ 2:1-23	☐ 3:1-31	☐ 4:1-24	☐ 5:1-31	☐ 6:1-40	☐ 7:1-25
33	☐ 8:1-35	☐ 9:1-57	☐ 10:1—11:40	☐ 12:1—13:25	☐ 14:1—15:20	☐ 16:1-31	☐ 17:1—18:31
34	☐ 19:1-30	☐ 20:1-48	☐ 21:1-25	☐ Ruth 1:1-22	☐ 2:1-23	☐ 3:1-18	☐ 4:1-22
35	☐ 1 Sam. 1:1-28	☐ 2:1-36	☐ 3:1—4:22	☐ 5:1—6:21	☐ 7:1—8:22	☐ 9:1-27	☐ 10:1—11:15
36	☐ 12:1—13:23	☐ 14:1-52	☐ 15:1-35	☐ 16:1-23	☐ 17:1-58	☐ 18:1-30	☐ 19:1-24
37	☐ 20:1-42	☐ 21:1—22:23	☐ 23:1—24:22	☐ 25:1-44	☐ 26:1-25	☐ 27:1—28:25	☐ 29:1—30:31
38	☐ 31:1-13	☐ 2 Sam. 1:1-27	☐ 2:1-32	☐ 3:1-39	☐ 4:1—5:25	☐ 6:1-23	☐ 7:1-29
39	☐ 8:1—9:13	☐ 10:1—11:27	☐ 12:1-31	☐ 13:1-39	☐ 14:1-33	☐ 15:1—16:23	☐ 17:1—18:33
40	☐ 19:1-43	☐ 20:1—21:22	☐ 22:1-51	☐ 23:1-39	☐ 24:1-25	☐ 1 Kings 1:1-19	☐ 1:20-53
41	☐ 2:1-46	☐ 3:1-28	☐ 4:1-34	☐ 5:1—6:38	☐ 7:1-22	☐ 7:23-51	☐ 8:1-36
42	☐ 8:37-66	☐ 9:1-28	☐ 10:1-29	☐ 11:1-43	☐ 12:1-33	☐ 13:1-34	☐ 14:1-31
43	☐ 15:1-34	☐ 16:1—17:24	☐ 18:1-46	☐ 19:1-21	☐ 20:1-43	☐ 21:1—22:53	☐ 2 Kings 1:1-18
44	☐ 2:1—3:27	☐ 4:1-44	☐ 5:1—6:33	☐ 7:1-20	☐ 8:1-29	☐ 9:1-37	☐ 10:1-36
45	☐ 11:1—12:21	☐ 13:1—14:29	☐ 15:1-38	☐ 16:1-20	☐ 17:1-41	☐ 18:1-37	☐ 19:1-37
46	☐ 20:1—21:26	☐ 22:1-20	☐ 23:1-37	☐ 24:1—25:30	☐ 1 Chron. 1:1-54	☐ 2:1—3:24	☐ 4:1—5:26
47	☐ 6:1-81	☐ 7:1-40	☐ 8:1-40	☐ 9:1-44	☐ 10:1—11:47	☐ 12:1-40	☐ 13:1—14:17
48	☐ 15:1—16:43	☐ 17:1-27	☐ 18:1—19:19	☐ 20:1—21:30	☐ 22:1—23:32	☐ 24:1—25:31	☐ 26:1-32
49	☐ 27:1-34	☐ 28:1—29:30	☐ 2 Chron. 1:1-17	☐ 2:1—3:17	☐ 4:1—5:14	☐ 6:1-42	☐ 7:1—8:18
50	☐ 9:1—10:19	☐ 11:1—12:16	☐ 13:1—15:19	☐ 16:1—17:19	☐ 18:1—19:11	☐ 20:1-37	☐ 21:1—22:12
51	☐ 23:1—24:27	☐ 25:1—26:23	☐ 27:1—28:27	☐ 29:1-36	☐ 30:1—31:21	☐ 32:1-33	☐ 33:1—34:33
52	☐ 35:1—36:23	☐ Ezra 1:1-11	☐ 2:1-70	☐ 3:1—4:24	☐ 5:1—6:22	☐ 7:1-28	☐ 8:1-36

Reading Schedule for the Recovery Version of the Old Testament with Footnotes

Wk.	Lord's Day	Monday	Tuesday	Wednesday	Thursday	Friday	Saturday
53	9:1—10:44 ☐	Neh. 1:1-11 ☐	2:1—3:32 ☐	4:1—5:19 ☐	6:1-19 ☐	7:1-73 ☐	8:1-18 ☐
54	9:1-20 ☐	9:21-38 ☐	10:1—11:36 ☐	12:1-47 ☐	13:1-31 ☐	Esth. 1:1-22 ☐	2:1—3:15 ☐
55	4:1—5:14 ☐	6:1—7:10 ☐	8:1-17 ☐	9:1—10:3 ☐	Job 1:1-22 ☐	2:1—3:26 ☐	4:1—5:27 ☐
56	6:1—7:21 ☐	8:1—9:35 ☐	10:1—11:20 ☐	12:1—13:28 ☐	14:1—15:35 ☐	16:1—17:16 ☐	18:1—19:29 ☐
57	20:1—21:34 ☐	22:1—23:17 ☐	24:1—25:6 ☐	26:1—27:23 ☐	28:1—29:25 ☐	30:1—31:40 ☐	32:1—33:33 ☐
58	34:1—35:16 ☐	36:1-33 ☐	37:1-24 ☐	38:1-41 ☐	39:1-30 ☐	40:1-24 ☐	41:1-34 ☐
59	42:1-17 ☐	Psa. 1:1-6 ☐	2:1—3:8 ☐	4:1—6:10 ☐	7:1—8:9 ☐	9:1—10:18 ☐	11:1—15:5 ☐
60	16:1—17:15 ☐	18:1-50 ☐	19:1—21:13 ☐	22:1-31 ☐	23:1—24:10 ☐	25:1—27:14 ☐	28:1—30:12 ☐
61	31:1—32:11 ☐	33:1—34:22 ☐	35:1—36:12 ☐	37:1-40 ☐	38:1—39:13 ☐	40:1—41:13 ☐	42:1—43:5 ☐
62	44:1-26 ☐	45:1-17 ☐	46:1—48:14 ☐	49:1—50:23 ☐	51:1—52:9 ☐	53:1—55:23 ☐	56:1—58:11 ☐
63	59:1—61:8 ☐	62:1—64:10 ☐	65:1—67:7 ☐	68:1-35 ☐	69:1—70:5 ☐	71:1—72:20 ☐	73:1—74:23 ☐
64	75:1—77:20 ☐	78:1-72 ☐	79:1—81:16 ☐	82:1—84:12 ☐	85:1—87:7 ☐	88:1—89:52 ☐	90:1—91:16 ☐
65	92:1—94:23 ☐	95:1—97:12 ☐	98:1—101:8 ☐	102:1—103:22 ☐	104:1—105:45 ☐	106:1-48 ☐	107:1-43 ☐
66	108:1—109:31 ☐	110:1—112:10 ☐	113:1—115:18 ☐	116:1—118:29 ☐	119:1-32 ☐	119:33-72 ☐	119:73-120 ☐
67	119:121-176 ☐	120:1—124:8 ☐	125:1—128:6 ☐	129:1—132:18 ☐	133:1—135:21 ☐	136:1—138:8 ☐	139:1—140:13 ☐
68	141:1—144:15 ☐	145:1—147:20 ☐	148:1—150:6 ☐	Prov. 1:1-33 ☐	2:1—3:35 ☐	4:1—5:23 ☐	6:1-35 ☐
69	7:1—8:36 ☐	9:1—10:32 ☐	11:1—12:28 ☐	13:1—14:35 ☐	15:1-33 ☐	16:1-33 ☐	17:1-28 ☐
70	18:1-24 ☐	19:1—20:30 ☐	21:1—22:29 ☐	23:1-35 ☐	24:1—25:28 ☐	26:1—27:27 ☐	28:1—29:27 ☐
71	30:1-33 ☐	31:1-31 ☐	Eccl. 1:1-18 ☐	2:1—3:22 ☐	4:1—5:20 ☐	6:1—7:29 ☐	8:1—9:18 ☐
72	10:1—11:10 ☐	12:1-14 ☐	S.S. 1:1-8 ☐	1:9-17 ☐	2:1-17 ☐	3:1-11 ☐	4:1-8 ☐
73	4:9-16 ☐	5:1-16 ☐	6:1-13 ☐	7:1-13 ☐	8:1-14 ☐	Isa. 1:1-11 ☐	1:12-31 ☐
74	2:1-22 ☐	3:1-26 ☐	4:1-6 ☐	5:1-30 ☐	6:1-13 ☐	7:1-25 ☐	8:1-22 ☐
75	9:1-21 ☐	10:1-34 ☐	11:1—12:6 ☐	13:1-22 ☐	14:1-14 ☐	14:15-32 ☐	15:1—16:14 ☐
76	17:1—18:7 ☐	19:1-25 ☐	20:1—21:17 ☐	22:1-25 ☐	23:1-18 ☐	24:1-23 ☐	25:1-12 ☐
77	26:1-21 ☐	27:1-13 ☐	28:1-29 ☐	29:1-24 ☐	30:1-33 ☐	31:1—32:20 ☐	33:1-24 ☐
78	34:1-17 ☐	35:1-10 ☐	36:1-22 ☐	37:1-38 ☐	38:1—39:8 ☐	40:1-31 ☐	41:1-29 ☐

Reading Schedule for the Recovery Version of the Old Testament with Footnotes

Wk.	Lord's Day	Monday	Tuesday	Wednesday	Thursday	Friday	Saturday
79	42:1-25 ☐	43:1-28 ☐	44:1-28 ☐	45:1-25 ☐	46:1-13 ☐	47:1-15 ☐	48:1-22 ☐
80	49:1-13 ☐	49:14-26 ☐	50:1—51:23 ☐	52:1-15 ☐	53:1-12 ☐	54:1-17 ☐	55:1-13 ☐
81	56:1-12 ☐	57:1-21 ☐	58:1-14 ☐	59:1-21 ☐	60:1-22 ☐	61:1-11 ☐	62:1-12 ☐
82	63:1-19 ☐	64:1-12 ☐	65:1-25 ☐	66:1-24 ☐	Jer. 1:1-19 ☐	2:1-19 ☐	2:20-37 ☐
83	3:1-25 ☐	4:1-31 ☐	5:1-31 ☐	6:1-30 ☐	7:1-34 ☐	8:1-22 ☐	9:1-26 ☐
84	10:1-25 ☐	11:1—12:17 ☐	13:1-27 ☐	14:1-22 ☐	15:1-21 ☐	16:1—17:27 ☐	18:1-23 ☐
85	19:1—20:18 ☐	21:1—22:30 ☐	23:1-40 ☐	24:1—25:38 ☐	26:1—27:22 ☐	28:1—29:32 ☐	30:1-24 ☐
86	31:1-23 ☐	31:24-40 ☐	32:1-44 ☐	33:1-26 ☐	34:1-22 ☐	35:1-19 ☐	36:1-32 ☐
87	37:1-21 ☐	38:1-28 ☐	39:1—40:16 ☐	41:1—42:22 ☐	43:1—44:30 ☐	45:1—46:28 ☐	47:1—48:16 ☐
88	48:17-47 ☐	49:1-22 ☐	49:23-39 ☐	50:1-27 ☐	50:28-46 ☐	51:1-27 ☐	51:28-64 ☐
89	52:1-34 ☐	Lam. 1:1-22 ☐	2:1-22 ☐	3:1-39 ☐	3:40-66 ☐	4:1-22 ☐	5:1-22 ☐
90	Ezek. 1:1-14 ☐	1:15-28 ☐	2:1—3:27 ☐	4:1—5:17 ☐	6:1—7:27 ☐	8:1—9:11 ☐	10:1—11:25 ☐
91	12:1—13:23 ☐	14:1—15:8 ☐	16:1-63 ☐	17:1—18:32 ☐	19:1-14 ☐	20:1-49 ☐	21:1-32 ☐
92	22:1-31 ☐	23:1-49 ☐	24:1-27 ☐	25:1—26:21 ☐	27:1-36 ☐	28:1-26 ☐	29:1—30:26 ☐
93	31:1—32:32 ☐	33:1-33 ☐	34:1-31 ☐	35:1—36:21 ☐	36:22-38 ☐	37:1-28 ☐	38:1—39:29 ☐
94	40:1-27 ☐	40:28-49 ☐	41:1-26 ☐	42:1—43:27 ☐	44:1-31 ☐	45:1-25 ☐	46:1-24 ☐
95	47:1-23 ☐	48:1-35 ☐	Dan. 1:1-21 ☐	2:1-30 ☐	2:31-49 ☐	3:1-30 ☐	4:1-37 ☐
96	5:1-31 ☐	6:1-28 ☐	7:1-12 ☐	7:13-28 ☐	8:1-27 ☐	9:1-27 ☐	10:1-21 ☐
97	11:1-22 ☐	11:23-45 ☐	12:1-13 ☐	Hosea 1:1-11 ☐	2:1-23 ☐	3:1—4:19 ☐	5:1-15 ☐
98	6:1-11 ☐	7:1-16 ☐	8:1-14 ☐	9:1-17 ☐	10:1-15 ☐	11:1-12 ☐	12:1-14 ☐
99	13:1—14:9 ☐	Joel 1:1-20 ☐	2:1-16 ☐	2:17-32 ☐	3:1-21 ☐	Amos 1:1-15 ☐	2:1-16 ☐
100	3:1-15 ☐	4:1—5:27 ☐	6:1—7:17 ☐	8:1—9:15 ☐	Obad. 1-21 ☐	Jonah 1:1-17 ☐	2:1—4:11 ☐
101	Micah 1:1-16 ☐	2:1—3:12 ☐	4:1—5:15 ☐	6:1—7:20 ☐	Nahum 1:1-15 ☐	2:1-13 ☐	Hab. 1:1-17 ☐
102	2:1-20 ☐	3:1-19 ☐	Zeph. 1:1-18 ☐	2:1-15 ☐	3:1-20 ☐	Hag. 1:1-15 ☐	2:1-23 ☐
103	Zech. 1:1-21 ☐	2:1-13 ☐	3:1-10 ☐	4:1-14 ☐	5:1—6:15 ☐	7:1—8:23 ☐	9:1-17 ☐
104	10:1—11:17 ☐	12:1—13:9 ☐	14:1-21 ☐	Mal. 1:1-14 ☐	2:1-17 ☐	3:1-18 ☐	4:1-6 ☐

Reading Schedule for the Recovery Version of the New Testament with Footnotes

Wk.	Lord's Day	Monday	Tuesday	Wednesday	Thursday	Friday	Saturday
1	Matt. 1:1-2 ☐	1:3-7 ☐	1:8-17 ☐	1:18-25 ☐	2:1-23 ☐	3:1-6 ☐	3:7-17 ☐
2	4:1-11 ☐	4:12-25 ☐	5:1-4 ☐	5:5-12 ☐	5:13-20 ☐	5:21-26 ☐	5:27-48 ☐
3	6:1-8 ☐	6:9-18 ☐	6:19-34 ☐	7:1-12 ☐	7:13-29 ☐	8:1-13 ☐	8:14-22 ☐
4	8:23-34 ☐	9:1-13 ☐	9:14-17 ☐	9:18-34 ☐	9:35—10:5 ☐	10:6-25 ☐	10:26-42 ☐
5	11:1-15 ☐	11:16-30 ☐	12:1-14 ☐	12:15-32 ☐	12:33-42 ☐	12:43—13:2 ☐	13:3-12 ☐
6	13:13-30 ☐	13:31-43 ☐	13:44-58 ☐	14:1-13 ☐	14:14-21 ☐	14:22-36 ☐	15:1-20 ☐
7	15:21-31 ☐	15:32-39 ☐	16:1-12 ☐	16:13-20 ☐	16:21-28 ☐	17:1-13 ☐	17:14-27 ☐
8	18:1-14 ☐	18:15-22 ☐	18:23-35 ☐	19:1-15 ☐	19:16-30 ☐	20:1-16 ☐	20:17-34 ☐
9	21:1-11 ☐	21:12-22 ☐	21:23-32 ☐	21:33-46 ☐	22:1-22 ☐	22:23-33 ☐	22:34-46 ☐
10	23:1-12 ☐	23:13-39 ☐	24:1-14 ☐	24:15-31 ☐	24:32-51 ☐	25:1-13 ☐	25:14-30 ☐
11	25:31-46 ☐	26:1-16 ☐	26:17-35 ☐	26:36-46 ☐	26:47-64 ☐	26:65-75 ☐	27:1-26 ☐
12	27:27-44 ☐	27:45-56 ☐	27:57—28:15 ☐	28:16-20 ☐	Mark 1:1 ☐	1:2-6 ☐	1:7-13 ☐
13	1:14-28 ☐	1:29-45 ☐	2:1-12 ☐	2:13-28 ☐	3:1-19 ☐	3:20-35 ☐	4:1-25 ☐
14	4:26-41 ☐	5:1-20 ☐	5:21-43 ☐	6:1-29 ☐	6:30-56 ☐	7:1-23 ☐	7:24-37 ☐
15	8:1-26 ☐	8:27—9:1 ☐	9:2-29 ☐	9:30-50 ☐	10:1-16 ☐	10:17-34 ☐	10:35-52 ☐
16	11:1-16 ☐	11:17-33 ☐	12:1-27 ☐	12:28-44 ☐	13:1-13 ☐	13:14-37 ☐	14:1-26 ☐
17	14:27-52 ☐	14:53-72 ☐	15:1-15 ☐	15:16-47 ☐	16:1-8 ☐	16:9-20 ☐	Luke 1:1-4 ☐
18	1:5-25 ☐	1:26-46 ☐	1:47-56 ☐	1:57-80 ☐	2:1-8 ☐	2:9-20 ☐	2:21-39 ☐
19	2:40-52 ☐	3:1-20 ☐	3:21-38 ☐	4:1-13 ☐	4:14-30 ☐	4:31-44 ☐	5:1-26 ☐
20	5:27—6:16 ☐	6:17-38 ☐	6:39-49 ☐	7:1-17 ☐	7:18-23 ☐	7:24-35 ☐	7:36-50 ☐
21	8:1-15 ☐	8:16-25 ☐	8:26-39 ☐	8:40-56 ☐	9:1-17 ☐	9:18-26 ☐	9:27-36 ☐
22	9:37-50 ☐	9:51-62 ☐	10:1-11 ☐	10:12-24 ☐	10:25-37 ☐	10:38-42 ☐	11:1-13 ☐
23	11:14-26 ☐	11:27-36 ☐	11:37-54 ☐	12:1-12 ☐	12:13-21 ☐	12:22-34 ☐	12:35-48 ☐
24	12:49-59 ☐	13:1-9 ☐	13:10-17 ☐	13:18-30 ☐	13:31—14:6 ☐	14:7-14 ☐	14:15-24 ☐
25	14:25-35 ☐	15:1-10 ☐	15:11-21 ☐	15:22-32 ☐	16:1-13 ☐	16:14-22 ☐	16:23-31 ☐
26	17:1-19 ☐	17:20-37 ☐	18:1-14 ☐	18:15-30 ☐	18:31-43 ☐	19:1-10 ☐	19:11-27 ☐

Reading Schedule for the Recovery Version of the New Testament with Footnotes

Wk.	Lord's Day	Monday	Tuesday	Wednesday	Thursday	Friday	Saturday
27	Luke 19:28-48 ☐	20:1-19 ☐	20:20-38 ☐	20:39—21:4 ☐	21:5-27 ☐	21:28-38 ☐	22:1-20 ☐
28	22:21-38 ☐	22:39-54 ☐	22:55-71 ☐	23:1-43 ☐	23:44-56 ☐	24:1-12 ☐	24:13-35 ☐
29	24:36-53 ☐	John 1:1-13 ☐	1:14-18 ☐	1:19-34 ☐	1:35-51 ☐	2:1-11 ☐	2:12-22 ☐
30	2:23—3:13 ☐	3:14-21 ☐	3:22-36 ☐	4:1-14 ☐	4:15-26 ☐	4:27-42 ☐	4:43-54 ☐
31	5:1-16 ☐	5:17-30 ☐	5:31-47 ☐	6:1-15 ☐	6:16-31 ☐	6:32-51 ☐	6:52-71 ☐
32	7:1-9 ☐	7:10-24 ☐	7:25-36 ☐	7:37-52 ☐	7:53—8:11 ☐	8:12-27 ☐	8:28-44 ☐
33	8:45-59 ☐	9:1-13 ☐	9:14-34 ☐	9:35—10:9 ☐	10:10-30 ☐	10:31—11:4 ☐	11:5-22 ☐
34	11:23-40 ☐	11:41-57 ☐	12:1-11 ☐	12:12-24 ☐	12:25-36 ☐	12:37-50 ☐	13:1-11 ☐
35	13:12-30 ☐	13:31-38 ☐	14:1-6 ☐	14:7-20 ☐	14:21-31 ☐	15:1-11 ☐	15:12-27 ☐
36	16:1-15 ☐	16:16-33 ☐	17:1-5 ☐	17:6-13 ☐	17:14-24 ☐	17:25—18:11 ☐	18:12-27 ☐
37	18:28-40 ☐	19:1-16 ☐	19:17-30 ☐	19:31-42 ☐	20:1-13 ☐	20:14-18 ☐	20:19-22 ☐
38	20:23-31 ☐	21:1-14 ☐	21:15-22 ☐	21:23-25 ☐	Acts 1:1-8 ☐	1:9-14 ☐	1:15-26 ☐
39	2:1-13 ☐	2:14-21 ☐	2:22-36 ☐	2:37-41 ☐	2:42-47 ☐	3:1-18 ☐	3:19—4:22 ☐
40	4:23-37 ☐	5:1-16 ☐	5:17-32 ☐	5:33-42 ☐	6:1—7:1 ☐	7:2-29 ☐	7:30-60 ☐
41	8:1-13 ☐	8:14-25 ☐	8:26-40 ☐	9:1-19 ☐	9:20-43 ☐	10:1-16 ☐	10:17-33 ☐
42	10:34-48 ☐	11:1-18 ☐	11:19-30 ☐	12:1-25 ☐	13:1-12 ☐	13:13-43 ☐	13:44—14:5 ☐
43	14:6-28 ☐	15:1-12 ☐	15:13-34 ☐	15:35—16:5 ☐	16:6-18 ☐	16:19-40 ☐	17:1-18 ☐
44	17:19-34 ☐	18:1-17 ☐	18:18-28 ☐	19:1-20 ☐	19:21-41 ☐	20:1-12 ☐	20:13-38 ☐
45	21:1-14 ☐	21:15-26 ☐	21:27-40 ☐	22:1-21 ☐	22:22-29 ☐	22:30—23:11 ☐	23:12-15 ☐
46	23:16-30 ☐	23:31—24:21 ☐	24:22—25:5 ☐	25:6-27 ☐	26:1-13 ☐	26:14-32 ☐	27:1-26 ☐
47	27:27—28:10 ☐	28:11-22 ☐	28:23-31 ☐	Rom. 1:1-2 ☐	1:3-7 ☐	1:8-17 ☐	1:18-25 ☐
48	1:26—2:10 ☐	2:11-29 ☐	3:1-20 ☐	3:21-31 ☐	4:1-12 ☐	4:13-25 ☐	5:1-11 ☐
49	5:12-17 ☐	5:18—6:5 ☐	6:6-11 ☐	6:12-23 ☐	7:1-12 ☐	7:13-25 ☐	8:1-2 ☐
50	8:3-6 ☐	8:7-13 ☐	8:14-25 ☐	8:26-39 ☐	9:1-18 ☐	9:19—10:3 ☐	10:4-15 ☐
51	10:16—11:10 ☐	11:11-22 ☐	11:23-36 ☐	12:1-3 ☐	12:4-21 ☐	13:1-14 ☐	14:1-12 ☐
52	14:13-23 ☐	15:1-13 ☐	15:14-33 ☐	16:1-5 ☐	16:6-24 ☐	16:25-27 ☐	1 Cor. 1:1-4 ☐

Reading Schedule for the Recovery Version of the New Testament with Footnotes

Wk.	Lord's Day	Monday	Tuesday	Wednesday	Thursday	Friday	Saturday
53	1 Cor. 1:5-9 ☐	1:10-17 ☐	1:18-31 ☐	2:1-5 ☐	2:6-10 ☐	2:11-16 ☐	3:1-9 ☐
54	3:10-13 ☐	3:14-23 ☐	4:1-9 ☐	4:10-21 ☐	5:1-13 ☐	6:1-11 ☐	6:12-20 ☐
55	7:1-16 ☐	7:17-24 ☐	7:25-40 ☐	8:1-13 ☐	9:1-15 ☐	9:16-27 ☐	10:1-4 ☐
56	10:5-13 ☐	10:14-33 ☐	11:1-6 ☐	11:7-16 ☐	11:17-26 ☐	11:27-34 ☐	12:1-11 ☐
57	12:12-22 ☐	12:23-31 ☐	13:1-13 ☐	14:1-12 ☐	14:13-25 ☐	14:26-33 ☐	14:34-40 ☐
58	15:1-19 ☐	15:20-28 ☐	15:29-34 ☐	15:35-49 ☐	15:50-58 ☐	16:1-9 ☐	16:10-24 ☐
59	2 Cor. 1:1-4 ☐	1:5-14 ☐	1:15-22 ☐	1:23—2:11 ☐	2:12-17 ☐	3:1-6 ☐	3:7-11 ☐
60	3:12-18 ☐	4:1-6 ☐	4:7-12 ☐	4:13-18 ☐	5:1-8 ☐	5:9-15 ☐	5:16-21 ☐
61	6:1-13 ☐	6:14—7:4 ☐	7:5-16 ☐	8:1-15 ☐	8:16-24 ☐	9:1-15 ☐	10:1-6 ☐
62	10:7-18 ☐	11:1-15 ☐	11:16-33 ☐	12:1-10 ☐	12:11-21 ☐	13:1-10 ☐	13:11-14 ☐
63	Gal. 1:1-5 ☐	1:6-14 ☐	1:15-24 ☐	2:1-13 ☐	2:14-21 ☐	3:1-4 ☐	3:5-14 ☐
64	3:15-22 ☐	3:23-29 ☐	4:1-7 ☐	4:8-20 ☐	4:21-31 ☐	5:1-12 ☐	5:13-21 ☐
65	5:22-26 ☐	6:1-10 ☐	6:11-15 ☐	6:16-18 ☐	Eph. 1:1-3 ☐	1:4-6 ☐	1:7-10 ☐
66	1:11-14 ☐	1:15-18 ☐	1:19-23 ☐	2:1-5 ☐	2:6-10 ☐	2:11-14 ☐	2:15-18 ☐
67	2:19-22 ☐	3:1-7 ☐	3:8-13 ☐	3:14-18 ☐	3:19-21 ☐	4:1-4 ☐	4:5-10 ☐
68	4:11-16 ☐	4:17-24 ☐	4:25-32 ☐	5:1-10 ☐	5:11-21 ☐	5:22-26 ☐	5:27-33 ☐
69	6:1-9 ☐	6:10-14 ☐	6:15-18 ☐	6:19-24 ☐	Phil. 1:1-7 ☐	1:8-18 ☐	1:19-26 ☐
70	1:27—2:4 ☐	2:5-11 ☐	2:12-16 ☐	2:17-30 ☐	3:1-6 ☐	3:7-11 ☐	3:12-16 ☐
71	3:17-21 ☐	4:1-9 ☐	4:10-23 ☐	Col. 1:1-8 ☐	1:9-13 ☐	1:14-23 ☐	1:24-29 ☐
72	2:1-7 ☐	2:8-15 ☐	2:16-23 ☐	3:1-4 ☐	3:5-15 ☐	3:16-25 ☐	4:1-18 ☐
73	1 Thes. 1:1-3 ☐	1:4-10 ☐	2:1-12 ☐	2:13—3:5 ☐	3:6-13 ☐	4:1-10 ☐	4:11—5:11 ☐
74	5:12-28 ☐	2 Thes. 1:1-12 ☐	2:1-17 ☐	3:1-18 ☐	1 Tim. 1:1-2 ☐	1:3-4 ☐	1:5-14 ☐
75	1:15-20 ☐	2:1-7 ☐	2:8-15 ☐	3:1-13 ☐	3:14—4:5 ☐	4:6-16 ☐	5:1-25 ☐
76	6:1-10 ☐	6:11-21 ☐	2 Tim. 1:1-10 ☐	1:11-18 ☐	2:1-15 ☐	2:16-26 ☐	3:1-13 ☐
77	3:14—4:8 ☐	4:9-22 ☐	Titus 1:1-4 ☐	1:5-16 ☐	2:1-15 ☐	3:1-8 ☐	3:9-15 ☐
78	Philem. 1:1-11 ☐	1:12-25 ☐	Heb. 1:1-2 ☐	1:3-5 ☐	1:6-14 ☐	2:1-9 ☐	2:10-18 ☐

Reading Schedule for the Recovery Version of the New Testament with Footnotes

Wk.	Lord's Day	Monday	Tuesday	Wednesday	Thursday	Friday	Saturday
79	Heb. 3:1-6 ☐	3:7-19 ☐	4:1-9 ☐	4:10-13 ☐	4:14-16 ☐	5:1-10 ☐	5:11—6:3 ☐
80	6:4-8 ☐	6:9-20 ☐	7:1-10 ☐	7:11-28 ☐	8:1-6 ☐	8:7-13 ☐	9:1-4 ☐
81	9:5-14 ☐	9:15-28 ☐	10:1-18 ☐	10:19-28 ☐	10:29-39 ☐	11:1-6 ☐	11:7-19 ☐
82	11:20-31 ☐	11:32-40 ☐	12:1-2 ☐	12:3-13 ☐	12:14-17 ☐	12:18-26 ☐	12:27-29 ☐
83	13:1-7 ☐	13:8-12 ☐	13:13-15 ☐	13:16-25 ☐	James 1:1-8 ☐	1:9-18 ☐	1:19-27 ☐
84	2:1-13 ☐	2:14-26 ☐	3:1-18 ☐	4:1-10 ☐	4:11-17 ☐	5:1-12 ☐	5:13-20 ☐
85	1 Pet. 1:1-2 ☐	1:3-4 ☐	1:5 ☐	1:6-9 ☐	1:10-12 ☐	1:13-17 ☐	1:18-25 ☐
86	2:1-3 ☐	2:4-8 ☐	2:9-17 ☐	2:18-25 ☐	3:1-13 ☐	3:14-22 ☐	4:1-6 ☐
87	4:7-16 ☐	4:17-19 ☐	5:1-4 ☐	5:5-9 ☐	5:10-14 ☐	2 Pet. 1:1-2 ☐	1:3-4 ☐
88	1:5-8 ☐	1:9-11 ☐	1:12-18 ☐	1:19-21 ☐	2:1-3 ☐	2:4-11 ☐	2:12-22 ☐
89	3:1-6 ☐	3:7-9 ☐	3:10-12 ☐	3:13-15 ☐	3:16 ☐	3:17-18 ☐	1 John 1:1-2 ☐
90	1:3-4 ☐	1:5 ☐	1:6 ☐	1:7 ☐	1:8-10 ☐	2:1-2 ☐	2:3-11 ☐
91	2:12-14 ☐	2:15-19 ☐	2:20-23 ☐	2:24-27 ☐	2:28-29 ☐	3:1-5 ☐	3:6-10 ☐
92	3:11-18 ☐	3:19-24 ☐	4:1-6 ☐	4:7-11 ☐	4:12-15 ☐	4:16—5:3 ☐	5:4-13 ☐
93	5:14-17 ☐	5:18-21 ☐	2 John 1:1-3 ☐	1:4-9 ☐	1:10-13 ☐	3 John 1:1-6 ☐	1:7-14 ☐
94	Jude 1:1-4 ☐	1:5-10 ☐	1:11-19 ☐	1:20-25 ☐	Rev. 1:1-3 ☐	1:4-6 ☐	1:7-11 ☐
95	1:12-13 ☐	1:14-16 ☐	1:17-20 ☐	2:1-6 ☐	2:7 ☐	2:8-9 ☐	2:10-11 ☐
96	2:12-14 ☐	2:15-17 ☐	2:18-23 ☐	2:24-29 ☐	3:1-3 ☐	3:4-6 ☐	3:7-9 ☐
97	3:10-13 ☐	3:14-18 ☐	3:19-22 ☐	4:1-5 ☐	4:6-7 ☐	4:8-11 ☐	5:1-6 ☐
98	5:7-14 ☐	6:1-8 ☐	6:9-17 ☐	7:1-8 ☐	7:9-17 ☐	8:1-6 ☐	8:7-12 ☐
99	8:13—9:11 ☐	9:12-21 ☐	10:1-4 ☐	10:5-11 ☐	11:1-4 ☐	11:5-14 ☐	11:15-19 ☐
100	12:1-4 ☐	12:5-9 ☐	12:10-18 ☐	13:1-10 ☐	13:11-18 ☐	14:1-5 ☐	14:6-12 ☐
101	14:13-20 ☐	15:1-8 ☐	16:1-12 ☐	16:13-21 ☐	17:1-6 ☐	17:7-18 ☐	18:1-8 ☐
102	18:9—19:4 ☐	19:5-10 ☐	19:11-16 ☐	19:17-21 ☐	20:1-6 ☐	20:7-10 ☐	20:11-15 ☐
103	21:1 ☐	21:2 ☐	21:3-8 ☐	21:9-13 ☐	21:14-18 ☐	21:19-21 ☐	21:22-27 ☐
104	22:1 ☐	22:2 ☐	22:3-11 ☐	22:12-15 ☐	22:16-17 ☐	22:18-21 ☐	

Week 7 — Day 4   Today's verses

Zech. For thus says Jehovah of hosts, After the
2:8-9 glory He has sent Me against the nations
who plunder you; for he who touches you
touches the pupil of His eye. For I am now
waving My hand over them, and they will
be plunder for those who served them; and
you will know that Jehovah of hosts has
sent Me.

_____
Date

Week 7 — Day 5   Today's verses

Matt. And Simon Peter answered and said, You
16:16 are the Christ, the Son of the living God.

1 Cor. But of Him you are in Christ Jesus, who be-
1:30 came wisdom to us from God: both righteousness and sanctification and redemption.

_____
Date

Week 7 — Day 6   Today's verses

1 Cor. For another foundation no one is able to
3:11 lay besides that which is laid, which is Jesus Christ.

Phil. To know Him and the power of His resur-
3:10 rection and the fellowship of His sufferings, being conformed to His death.

_____
Date

Week 7 — Day 1   Today's verses

1 Cor. Do you not know that you are the temple
3:16 of God, and _that_ the Spirit of God dwells
in you?

Rev. And I saw no temple in it, for the Lord
21:22 God the Almighty and the Lamb are its
temple.

_____
Date

Week 7 — Day 2   Today's verses

Zech. ...Thus speaks Jehovah of hosts, saying,
6:12-13 Here is a man, whose name is the Shoot;
and he will shoot forth from his place and
will build the temple of Jehovah. Indeed,...
he will bear majesty and will sit and rule on
his throne; and he will be a priest on his
throne; and the counsel of peace will be between the two of them.

_____
Date

Week 7 — Day 3   Today's verses

Zech. I saw during the night, and behold, a man
1:8 was riding upon a red horse; and He was
standing among the myrtle trees that were
in the bottoms; and behind Him there were
red, reddish-brown, and white horses.

16 Therefore thus says Jehovah, I return to Jerusalem with compassions; My house will
be built in it, declares Jehovah of hosts,
and a measuring line will be stretched
over Jerusalem.

_____
Date

Week 8 — Day 1 — Today's verses

1 Cor. For another foundation no one is able to
3:11 lay besides that which is laid, which is Jesus Christ.

1 Pet. Coming to Him, a living stone, rejected by
2:4-5 men but with God chosen *and* precious, you yourselves also, as living stones, are being built up as a spiritual house...

Date

Week 8 — Day 2 — Today's verses

Eph. Being built upon the foundation of the
2:20 apostles and prophets, Christ Jesus Himself being the cornerstone.

Zech. For here is the stone that I have set before
3:9 Joshua—upon one stone are seven eyes. I will engrave its engraving, declares Jehovah of hosts, and I will remove the iniquity of that land in one day.

Date

Week 8 — Day 3 — Today's verses

Zech. ...These seven rejoice when they see the
4:10 plummet in the hand of Zerubbabel; they are the eyes of Jehovah running to and fro on the whole earth.

Rev. And I saw in the midst of the throne...
5:6 a Lamb standing as having *just* been slain, having seven horns and seven eyes, which are the seven Spirits of God sent forth into all the earth.

Date

Week 8 — Day 4 — Today's verses

John And the Word became flesh and tabernac-
1:14 led among us (and we beheld His glory, glory as of the only Begotten from the Father), full of grace and reality.

16 For of His fullness we have all received, and grace upon grace.

2 Cor. The grace of the Lord Jesus Christ and the love
13:14 of God and the fellowship of the Holy Spirit be with you all.

Date

Week 8 — Day 5 — Today's verses

1 John Beloved, now we are children of God, and
3:2 it has not yet been manifested what we will be. We know that if He is manifested, we will be like Him because we will see Him even as He is.

S.S. You are as beautiful, my love, as Tirzah,
6:4 as lovely as Jerusalem, as terrible as an army with banners.

13 Return, return, O Shulammite; return, return, that we may gaze at you. Why should you gaze at the Shulammite, as upon the dance of two camps?

Date

Week 8 — Day 6 — Today's verses

John In My Father's house are many abodes; if *it*
14:2 *were not so*, I would have told you; for I go to prepare a place for you.

Rev. And I saw the holy city, New Jerusalem,
21:2-3 coming down out of heaven from God, prepared as a bride adorned for her husband. And I heard a loud voice out of the throne, saying, Behold, the tabernacle of God is with men, and He will tabernacle with them...

Date

Week 9 — Day 4 Today's verses

Zech. ...Upon one stone are seven eyes....And I
3:9 will remove the iniquity of that land in one day.

4:10 ...For these seven rejoice when they see the plummet in the hand of Zerubbabel; they are the eyes of Jehovah running to and fro on the whole earth.

Rev. And I saw...a Lamb standing as having
5:6 just been slain, having...seven eyes, which are the seven Spirits of God sent forth into all the earth.

_____
Date

Week 9 — Day 5 Today's verses

Rev. ...And there were seven lamps of fire burn-
4:5 ing before the throne, which are the seven Spirits of God.

22:1 And he showed me a river of water of life, bright as crystal, proceeding out of the throne of God and of the Lamb in the middle of its street.

_____
Date

Week 9 — Day 6 Today's verses

Zech. And there are two olive trees beside it,
4:3 one to the right of the bowl and one to the left.

12, 14 ...What are the two olive branches that are by the side of the two golden spouts, which empty the gold from themselves?...And he said, These are the two sons of oil, who stand by the Lord of the whole earth.

_____
Date

Week 9 — Day 1 Today's verses

Zech. And he said to me, What do you see? And
4:2 I said, I see that there is a lampstand all of gold, with its bowl on top of it and its seven lamps upon it, with seven pipes for each of the lamps on top of it.

Rev. And out of the throne come forth light-
4:5 nings and voices and thunders. And there were seven lamps of fire burning before the throne, which are the seven Spirits of God.

_____
Date

Week 9 — Day 2 Today's verses

Zech. ...There is a lampstand all of gold;...and
4:2-3 there are two olive trees beside it, one to the right of the bowl and one to the left.

6 ...This is the word of Jehovah to Zerubbabel, saying, Not by might nor by power, but by My Spirit, says Jehovah of hosts.

_____
Date

Week 9 — Day 3 Today's verses

1 Cor. For also in one Spirit we were all baptized
12:13 into one Body, whether Jews or Greeks, whether slaves or free, and were all given to drink one Spirit.

Gal. I am crucified with Christ; and it is no
2:20 longer I who live, but it is Christ who lives in me; and the life which I now live in the flesh I live in faith, the faith of the Son of God, who loved me and gave Himself up for me.

_____
Date

Week 10 — Day 4   Today's verses

Zech. Exult greatly, O daughter of Zion; shout,
9:9-10 O daughter of Jerusalem! Now your King comes to you. He is righteous and bears salvation, lowly and riding upon a donkey, even upon a colt, the foal of a donkey;... and He will speak peace unto the nations, and His dominion will be from sea to sea and from the River unto the ends of the earth.

_____
Date

Week 10 — Day 5   Today's verses

Zech. Then I lifted up my eyes and looked, and
1:18 there were four horns.

20-21 Then Jehovah showed me four craftsmen. And I said, What do these come to do? And he spoke, saying, These are the horns that have so scattered Judah that no man lifts up his head, but these have come to terrify them, to cast down the horns of the nations who have lifted up the horn against the land of Judah to scatter it.

_____
Date

Week 10 — Day 6   Today's verses

2 Thes. For *it is* the mystery of lawlessness *that*
2:7-8 is now operating, *but* only until the one now restraining goes out of the way. And then the lawless one will be revealed (whom the Lord Jesus will slay by the breath of His mouth and bring to nothing by the manifestation of His coming).

_____
Date

Week 10 — Day 1   Today's verses

Zech. The burden of the word of Jehovah con-
12:1 cerning Israel. *Thus* declares Jehovah, who stretches forth the heavens and lays the foundations of the earth and forms the spirit of man within him.

John God is Spirit, and those who worship Him
4:24 must worship in spirit and truthfulness.

1 Cor. But the spiritual man discerns all things, but
2:15 he himself is discerned by no one.

_____
Date

Week 10 — Day 2   Today's verses

Zech. Then I lifted up my eyes and I looked, and
2:1-2 there was a man, and in His hand was a measuring line. And I said, Where are you going? And He said to me, To measure Jerusalem; to see how great its breadth is and how great its length is.

5 For I will be her wall of fire round about, declares Jehovah, and I will be the glory within her.

_____
Date

Week 10 — Day 3   Today's verses

Zech. So I shepherded the flock of slaughter,
11:7 and thereby the afflicted of the flock. And I took to myself two staffs; one I called Favor, and the other I called Bonds; and I shepherded the flock.

10:8 I will whistle for them and gather them, for I have redeemed them; and they will multiply as they have multiplied.

_____
Date

Week 11 — Day 4   **Today's verses**

Luke 10:41-42 — ...The Lord answered and said to her, Martha, Martha, you are anxious and troubled about many things; but there is need of one thing, for Mary has chosen the good part, which shall not be taken away from her.

Date

Week 11 — Day 1   **Today's verses**

Rev. 18:2 — And He cried with a strong voice, saying, Fallen, fallen is Babylon the Great! And she has become a dwelling place of demons and a hold of every unclean spirit and a hold of every unclean and hateful bird.

2 Pet. 1:4 — Through which He has granted to us precious and exceedingly great promises that through these you might become partakers of the divine nature, having escaped the corruption which is in the world by lust.

Date

Week 11 — Day 5   **Today's verses**

Phil. 3:7-8 — ...What things were gains to me, these I have counted as loss on account of Christ. But moreover I also count all things to be loss on account of the excellency of the knowledge of Christ Jesus my Lord, on account of whom I have suffered the loss of all things and count *them* as refuse that I may gain Christ.

Date

Week 11 — Day 2   **Today's verses**

Matt. 19:27 — Then Peter answered and said to Him, Behold, we have left all and followed You. What then will there be for us?

Date

Week 11 — Day 6   **Today's verses**

Matt. 13:45-46 — Again, the kingdom of the heavens is like a merchant seeking fine pearls; and finding one pearl of great value, he went and sold all that he had and bought it.

Acts 20:28 — Take heed to yourselves and to all the flock, among whom the Holy Spirit has placed you as overseers to shepherd the church of God, which He obtained through His own blood.

Date

Week 11 — Day 3   **Today's verses**

Luke 16:13 — No household servant can serve two masters; for either he will hate the one and love the other, or he will hold to one and despise the other. You cannot serve God and mammon.

Heb. 13:5 — Let your way of life be without the love of money, being satisfied with the things which are at hand; for He Himself has said, "I shall by no means give you up, neither by any means shall I abandon you."

Date

Week 12 — Day 1   Today's verses

Zech. ...Thus speaks Jehovah of hosts, saying, Here
6:12-13 is a man, whose name is the Shoot; and he
will shoot forth from his place and will build
the temple of Jehovah. Indeed, it is he who
will build the temple of Jehovah; and he will
bear majesty and will sit and rule on his
throne; and he will be a priest on his throne;
and the counsel of peace will be between
the two of them.

Date

Week 12 — Day 2   Today's verses

Psa. Jehovah has sworn, and He will not change:
110:4 You are a Priest forever according to the order of Melchizedek.

Heb. Now in the things which are being said the
8:1-2 chief point is this: We have such a High
Priest, who sat down on the right hand of the
throne of the Majesty in the heavens, a Minister of the holy places, even of the true tabernacle, which the Lord pitched, not man.

Date

Week 12 — Day 3   Today's verses

Heb. ...It is according to the likeness of Mel-
7:15-16 chizedek that a different Priest arises, who
has been appointed not according to the
law of a fleshy commandment but according to the power of an indestructible
life.

25 Hence also He is able to save to the uttermost those who come forward to God
through Him, since He lives always to intercede for them.

Date

Week 12 — Day 4   Today's verses

Rev. ...Jesus Christ, the faithful Witness, the
1:5-6 Firstborn of the dead, and the Ruler of the
kings of the earth. To Him who loves us
and has released us from our sins by His
blood and made us a kingdom, priests...

20:6 Blessed and holy is he who has part in the
first resurrection;...they will be priests of
God and of Christ and will reign with Him
for a thousand years.

Date

Week 12 — Day 5   Today's verses

Rev. And he showed me a river of water of life,
22:1 bright as crystal, proceeding out of the throne
of God and of the Lamb in the middle of
its street.

1 Pet. But you are a chosen race, a royal priest-
2:9 hood, a holy nation, a people acquired for a
possession, so that you may tell out the virtues of Him who has called you out of darkness into His marvelous light.

Date

Week 12 — Day 6   Today's verses

Heb. Let us therefore come forward with bold-
4:16 ness to the throne of grace that we may receive mercy and find grace for timely help.

1 Pet. You yourselves also, as living stones, are
2:5 being built up as a spiritual house into a
holy priesthood to offer up spiritual sacrifices acceptable to God through Jesus
Christ.

Date